P9-AQD-030

Double Wedding Ring
QUILTS
TRADITIONS MADE MODERN

Full-Circle Sketches from Life

Victoria Findlay Wolfe

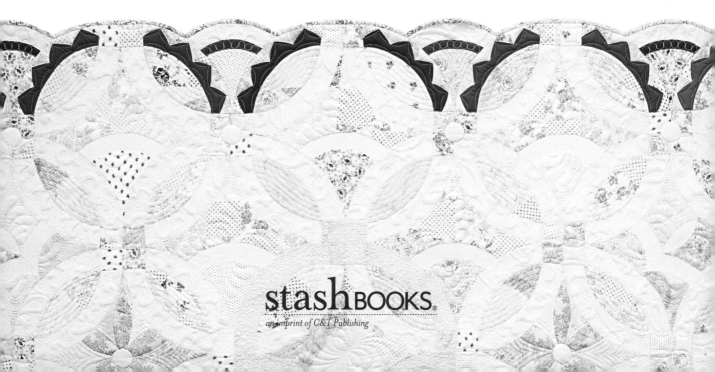

stashBOOKS
an imprint of C&T Publishing

Text copyright © 2015 by Victoria Findlay Wolfe

Photography and Artwork copyright © 2015 by C&T Publishing, Inc.

Publisher: Amy Marson

Creative Director: Gailen Runge

Art Director: Kristy Zacharias

Editor: Liz Aneloski

Technical Editors: Debbie Rodgers, Mary E. Flynn, and Nan Powell

Cover/Book Designer: April Mostek

Production Coordinator: Zinnia Heinzmann and Freesia Pearson Blizard

Production Editor: Alice Mace Nakanishi

Illustrator: Mary E. Flynn

Photo Assistant: Mary Peyton Peppo

Style photography by Nissa Brehmer and instructional photography by Diane Pedersen of C&T Publishing, unless otherwise noted below:

• Photos by Victoria Findlay Wolfe: pages 9, 13, 21, 33, 40 left, 80, and 87 bottom

• Photos by Katherine Slingluff: pages 4, 11 bottom, 14 top, 41, 61, 62, 71, 72, 74, 82, 83, 99, 100, and 111

• Photos by Monica Buck: page 108

Published by Stash Books, an imprint of C&T Publishing, Inc., P.O. Box 1456, Lafayette, CA 94549

All rights reserved. No part of this work covered by the copyright hereon may be used in any form or reproduced by any means—graphic, electronic, or mechanical, including photocopying, recording, taping, or information storage and retrieval systems—without written permission from the publisher. The copyrights on individual artworks are retained by the artists as noted in *Double Wedding Ring Quilts—Traditions Made Modern*. These designs may be used to make items only for personal use. Donations to nonprofit groups, items for sale, or items for display only at events require the following credit on a conspicuous label: Designs copyright © 2015 by Victoria Findlay Wolfe from the book *Double Wedding Ring Quilts—Traditions Made Modern* from C&T Publishing, Inc. Permission for all other purposes must be requested in writing from C&T Publishing, Inc.

Attention Copy Shops: Please note the following exception—publisher and author give permission to photocopy pages 106 and 107 and pattern pullout pages P1 and P2 for personal use only.

Attention Teachers: C&T Publishing, Inc., encourages you to use this book as a text for teaching. Contact us at 800-284-1114 or ctpub.com for lesson plans and information about the C&T Creative Troupe.

We take great care to ensure that the information included in our products is accurate and presented in good faith, but no warranty is provided nor are results guaranteed. Having no control over the choices of materials or procedures used, neither the author nor C&T Publishing, Inc., shall have any liability to any person or entity with respect to any loss or damage caused directly or indirectly by the information contained in this book. For your convenience, we post an up-to-date listing of corrections on our website (ctpub.com). If a correction is not already noted, please contact our customer service department at ctinfo@ctpub.com or at P.O. Box 1456, Lafayette, CA 94549.

Trademark (™) and registered trademark (®) names are used throughout this book. Rather than use the symbols with every occurrence of a trademark or registered trademark name, we are using the names only in the editorial fashion and to the benefit of the owner, with no intention of infringement.

Library of Congress Cataloging-in-Publication Data

Wolfe, Victoria Findlay, 1970-

Double wedding ring quilts : traditions made modern : full-circle sketches from life / Victoria Findlay Wolfe.

pages cm

ISBN 978-1-61745-026-6 (soft cover)

1. Patchwork--Patterns. 2. Quilting--Patterns. 3. Double wedding ring quilts. I. Title.

TT835.W6423 2015

746.46--dc23

2014022717

Printed in China

10 9 8 7 6 5 4 3 2 1

Dedication

To my darling daughter, Beatrice.

Had you not come into my life,

I might not have found my passion.

You are the greatest joy in my life.

Acknowledgments

I'd like to thank all the wonderful quilters, like my grandmother, Elda Wolfe, who before me, made beautiful memories through textiles.

I'd also like to thank all today's quilters and friends, who have told their stories through quilts that inspire me to continue to "make."

Specifically and humbly, I thank these people for being a part of my daily inspiration:

Kim Hryniewicz

Roderick Kiracofe

Susan Wernecke

Michele Muska

Shelly Pagliai

Debby Ritenbaugh Brown

Karen McTavish

Lisa Sipes

Linda Sekerak

The C&T staff

My SSQ pals (you know who you are)

My fabulous husband, Michael Findlay, I love you.

A big thanks to these companies:

AccuQuilt

Aurifil

Havel's Sewing

Juki International

Reliable Corporation

Robert Kaufman Fabrics

Triangles on a Roll

CONTENTS

FOREWORD

by Roderick Kiracofe

What if you had a grandmother you loved very much and have extremely happy memories of time spent at her home in southwest Minnesota? You watched her make quilts and sew and crochet and work with your grandfather in the vegetable and flower garden. What if you decide to take a closer look at the quilt you just made but don't like; and you decide to cut it up, rearrange the pieces, shift it all around, get a new perspective? And then the "Aha!" moment happens. This is what happened for contemporary quiltmaker/artist Victoria Findlay Wolfe in 2012, and the result was *Double-Edged Love* (page 12). This quilt led to the creation and the working through of many personal memories of growing up in the Midwest, her connections with her family, especially her beloved grandmother, and time spent growing up on the farm.

Double-Edged Love clearly struck a chord with many who saw it for the first time at QuiltCon in 2013, the first national conference the Modern Quilt Guild, organized and hosted in Austin, Texas. In fact, the quilt won Best in Show. It also opened up something unexpectedly for Victoria.

Let's step back a little and look at the pattern that is the basis for starting Victoria on her personal journey. Like much of quilt history and the origins of and names attached to quilt patterns, it is ever evolving. Speculation, mystery, and myth remain alongside good solid research and knowledge. The Wedding Ring pattern is no exception. Known as Single Wedding Ring, Double Wedding Ring, or Wedding Ring, did it evolve from earlier patterns Pine Burr, Pickle Dish, or Indian Wedding Ring? Most likely, yes.

We do know that the Double Wedding Ring pattern was first published in *Capper's Weekly* in Kansas on October 20, 1928. Shortly after, the *Weekly Kansas City Star* and then the *Kansas City Star* published patterns by Ruby Short McKim. However, it wasn't until 1931 that she actually called it Double Wedding Ring. By 1931, the pattern spread like wildfire throughout the Midwest and across the country. Patterns, instructions, and the actual cut pieces of fabric were available through syndicated pattern services and cottage businesses to supply the eager quiltmaker wanting to try her hand at this popular quilt.

Speculation is that the pattern had already gained popularity on its own and was shared among quiltmakers who mailed their own patterns to each other years before the newspapers actually began to publish and promote the pattern.

I was intrigued by a notation I came across in the valuable research Wilene Smith compiled on this pattern. She noted that quilt historian Merikay Waldvogel discovered a Double Wedding Ring made in Georgia reportedly around 1900. This would be a very early example, but it is not the date that intrigued

me most, but the name that the family had always called the quilt: *Tangled Love*. There are so many interpretations, subtle and not-so-subtle meanings, of what tangled love could and did mean to those family members. As we know, all quilts come with multiple stories and meanings surrounding the maker and those who lived with and slept under what the makers have made.

This brings me back to Victoria's body of twelve quilts in this series and the layers, stories, memories, and subtle or hidden messages embedded in them. Here we have a living maker who can and has documented her stories and thoughts about her creations. My guess is that with all quiltmakers, some of those stories remain untold, but how can they not be reflected within the quilt? Journeys—from farm to grandparents' home; from small town to the big city; the many joys of childhood and carefree times at grandmother's house; being taught to make, sew, build, garden, and create. Happy times—Christmas, family, friends. Emotions, thoughts, and decisions—joy, sorrow, pain, love, disappointment, elation, enthusiasm, idealism, being practical, doors opening, paths taken, choices made, surprises, success and failure. All these things make up a life.

From the memories, associations, and encounters of a life come the fabrics and materials that make up the actual pieces.

Like so many quiltmakers before her, Victoria loves fabrics—and a vast array of them. She uses old clothing, secondhand-store finds, polyester double knits (like those her grandmother used), her scrap bag, as well as the latest and trendiest fabrics available.

As I spoke with Victoria and viewed the twelve very beautiful and unique quilts, I was struck by the connection and bond she has with the generations of quiltmakers before her, but particularly to Nancy Crow and her work with the traditional Double Wedding Ring. Nancy also became intrigued by this pattern and was drawn to create her interpretations in six quilts, which she titled *Double Mexican Wedding Rings*.

It is amazing how, by starting with something we don't like or aren't pleased with and then stepping back (sometimes with drastic measures involving scissors), we gain a new perspective and see things differently. Like the circles that make up these quilts, Victoria took this approach and has come full circle with many aspects and pieces of her life to create a stunning body of work.

—Roderick Kiracofe
Author of *Unconventional & Unexpected: American Quilts below the Radar 1950–2000* and co-author of *The American Quilt: A History of Cloth and Comfort 1750–1950.* He is also an artist and art collector and lives in San Francisco, California.

INTRODUCTION

Exploring the Double Wedding Ring

Little did I know that making one quilt would set me off on a wild Double Wedding Ring adventure! That I would teach myself a thing or two about my own process is such a treat! I used to work very quickly, not contemplate too long over my choices. I would let my intuition take me on the journey and be thrilled to move on and start a new quilt. I still do this sometimes, but I can now sit and stay with a project for greater lengths of time, and build—not just more complicated quilts but quilts with a stronger connection to who I am.

This book, although a very personal journey for me in realizing and embracing respect for my roots, is actually the "next step" in improvisational quilting. My first book, *15 Minutes of Play—Improvisational Quilts*, explores how to get you to play, to create a connection to your creativity, and to encourage you to ask all the right questions to make those personal connections to your work. In this book, *Double Wedding Ring Quilts—Traditions Made Modern*, we will look at a traditional platform to begin with and see how we can push the limits, place a bit more of ourselves into the quilt, add our story, and push our skills into a new realm, while making personal connections that relate to our past.

After all, creativity is making our skill set, knowledge, and personal connections strike the same chord all at once. When that happens—lights flash and we have that electric rush of "Aha!"—that's it!

Victoria with *Double Edged Love* (page 12), awarded Best in Show, QuiltCon 2013

We know already how to play in our scraps. Now look at what we are making by using new eyes on old projects. But what if we look at *one* pattern, change one thing each time we try it, and see where that play will lead us next?

Don't Sweat the Small Stuff

I am a very big believer in not worrying about making mistakes. I have found through making more than 400 quilts that making a mistake is, of course, a great learning experience and can be the perfect design challenge! Turn that mistake into a design decision, and take the "oopsie" and make it the star of the quilt. Those moments are the perfect opportunity to push your creativity.

Making a mistake, or learning a new skill and finding you are not perfect, should not deter you from trying it again.

Making a mistake, or learning a new skill and finding you are not perfect, should not deter you from trying it again. *No one* makes *perfect* quilts. The more you make and practice, the better your quilts will be! Your own personal best is good enough. If you strive to do better, then go for it. I have found that by just continuing to make, my skills get better naturally. I say that aloud to myself, as I am learning to use my longarm machine ... (see, we all have things to work on!).

Change One Thing

In my classes, I often hear people say, "Improvisation is hard for me; I only make pattern quilts." And this is where I remind them that the "15 Minutes of Play" is just the exercise they need to break a task into a small amount of time, so they can try something new. Just a few minutes of time is the trick you need to approach your fabrics in a new way, with new eyes, and wait for the fabrics to speak to you. Also, I encourage people to change just one thing. One tiny change can open your creative eyes to bigger and greater design opportunities!

SO HOW DO YOU DO THAT?

Make a list of the skills and techniques you have and consider the templates and tools you have to play with.

▶ Can you add some Made-Fabric somewhere? (I use the term "Made-Fabric" to describe my improvisationally pieced scrap fabric.)

▶ Can you add a half-square triangle in the design?

▶ What if you stitch-and-flip a new color somewhere into the pattern?

▶ Have you tried using interesting fabrics? Stripes, solids, dots ...

▶ How about ombré fabrics, gradated fabrics that go from light to dark? How can that change the pattern?

▶ How can you deal with or accentuate the negative space?

▶ Can you play with the placement of the lights and darks in the block pattern?

▶ Can you add a few different values of one color?

▶ Can you add a humility block (a block you made a mistake on), just because?

Push It Further

By exploring *all your options* you will find a few tricks that have led you to unexpected delights in your process. Slow down. *Look* at each block and find that one thing you can change.

In this book, I want to show you how making one quilt changed my process, again. Each time I played with a template and tried one thing new, it gave me many more new ideas. Ultimately, this gave me a whole new understanding of and respect for where I came from; who I am now; and where I am going as a quilter, an artist, and an overall human being. I hope I can inspire you to look and find more ideas and joy in your creative process!

Forever Garden, Victoria Findlay Wolfe, 2013, 41″ × 41″

Joy

I have found through my quiltmaking that I quilt *joy*. These quilts are all about happy memories from my childhood, based around my grandparents, Elda and Leo Wolfe. Their home, in a small southern Minnesota town on the Mississippi, was so different from the way I grew up. It was the happiest place for me to be as a kid.

Memories: their beautiful gardens, fresh canned food, the yummy homemade smell that hits you when you entered their home, swinging on the glider on the screened-in porch watching cars drive by, Christmases filled with fresh baked goodies, bicycling around town with my cousins, or running to the store to buy candy. All these things made visiting my grandparents the ideal summer and holiday vacations that I get nostalgic for to this day. Perhaps through pushing *play* further, you too will be able to see different ways to add flavors and traditions of your past that can help you make quilts that are truly and uniquely you.

Double-Edged
LOVE

Everything started with this quilt. One day I am sewing along, making and playing. I place one fabric next to another, and I have a visual memory of my grandparents and farm fields. I place the next fabric and I see New York City streets. A creative connection is made! I can now see how they relate. I start making those creative connections to past memories, and tiny, creative flashbulbs are giving me those "Aha!" moments of exhilaration! Let me explain further. ...

When I first received a bundle of Center City fabrics from Jay McCarroll, I really had no idea what I would make with them for weeks. Finally, I thought, *Just open the fat quarters and stick them up on your design wall to see what you have to work with.*

I left them there for a week or so before I decided to just work with what I knew

Risk taking — it is great for your creativity!

I liked. Often, if I am stuck, I look at the fabrics for a while to find three things I like about them. Maybe it is a print, a color, or a combination that happens by the placement on the wall. Then I go from there. ... I do not worry about making mistakes; I stick with what I know.

First, I noticed the pink/red and purple peeking out of the fabrics, and I loved the black of the buildings. So that was my starting point. What if I slashed those fat quarters randomly, inserting different widths of black strips? Making the first cut without a plan is often the hardest part of pushing your creativity. Risk taking—it is great for your creativity! Let go! I could have made a big fat mess, and well, maybe I did. ... I made those fat quarters into a quilt top and decided, no, it was not working for me. So what's next?

Well, as I stood again, looking, I saw New York City streets within the patterns, and I very quickly decided *that* was my first step. How else could I divide that space to break up the block divisions I had made?

What if I cut that top apart by rolling it through the AccuQuilt die cutter using my Double Wedding Ring die? Okay, done! Immediately I had a "Yes!" feeling. I noticed that within each ring, parts felt like aerial views of the farmland in Minnesota, and other parts still looked like NYC. Hmmm, I began to see a full-circle moment. Combining where I am from with where I am now is a great place to start. I've made visual connections from the past with today's life, and I can continue to make sight, sound, and smell connections to boost my creative think tank. The brain is great at linking concepts through memory—we just need to *feed* it a bit to get those fires burning!

So how do you keep going on that theme, building a quilt that represents the space and time between life events, while rattling around some old memories? Think of your joyful memories. Think about the smells, the textures, the sounds. Place yourself in the context of the year, your age, all that was happening around you. Many of the random thoughts you conjure will encourage your brain to make odd connections, and new ideas will be born. The next step is to take action!

While making this quilt, I was focusing on the space between my grandmother's work and my own, and the bond between the two of us: How do Minnesota and New York relate? How do I make a modern quilt yet keep it based in the traditions of quilting? I felt that the Double Wedding Ring pattern was doing most of that work for me, so how could I change the pattern without distorting it? How could I bring the two worlds together and have parts of the design disappear, which really represents that time in my life when I was struggling to find who I was as an artist and as a woman. Phew! Big questions!

Some of those times were sad and difficult (black), others were fun and exciting yet a bit naive (pink), and at times things just fell into place and were spot on (red!). Colors represent what I like. I chose the colors that I liked in the fabrics; I went with what I knew, trusting my intuition to make it work.

When I make a quilt, I make it for me and to my taste. One thing I learned about making this quilt is that it wasn't just about those fabrics anymore—it was about all the connections I was making personally for myself, accepting who I am, where I came from, and where I will go from here.

I have a fine art degree. I was trained as a painter, and the difference between how I paint and how I quilt is that I was painting the sadness in my life—my emotions were always on my sleeve when I worked in paint. My art had something to tell. But when I quilt, I am totally focused on the *joy*. A quilt is about being hugged, warmed, and comforted. I love that usefulness that a quilt can provide. It is also how I keep my traditional quilting roots connected to my past. I need to make, to be useful—a trait I learned growing up on that farm in Minnesota. You make, you create, you grow, you reap, you preserve, you cook, and you eat. So I make, I sew, I cut, I keep warm, and I give comfort. All these things lead to joy.

THE GOAL

▸ Use three elements I liked about the fabrics (pink, red, and black).

▸ Work with the "mistake"; use it as a jumping-off point.

▸ Use my tools; the AccuQuilt GO! Fabric Cutter Double Wedding Ring templates saved this quilt from being another unfinished quilt top.

ADD LAYERS

▸ Start simple and push it further by adding more details.

▸ Pay attention to personal connections (farm, city streets, traditional, modern).

▸ Play up the connections; take action!

▸ Look at how to add negative space.

▸ Relate the chaos of New York City streets —dotted lines of pavement markings.

PUSH IT FURTHER

▸ Ask a lot of questions! Stir that pot of emotions and memories!

▸ Make the thought complete, and then add a few extra skills.

▸ Appliqué elements to accentuate some design elements.

▸ Add hand quilting to bring traditional and modern together.

▸ Carry the thoughts all the way to the backing and binding.

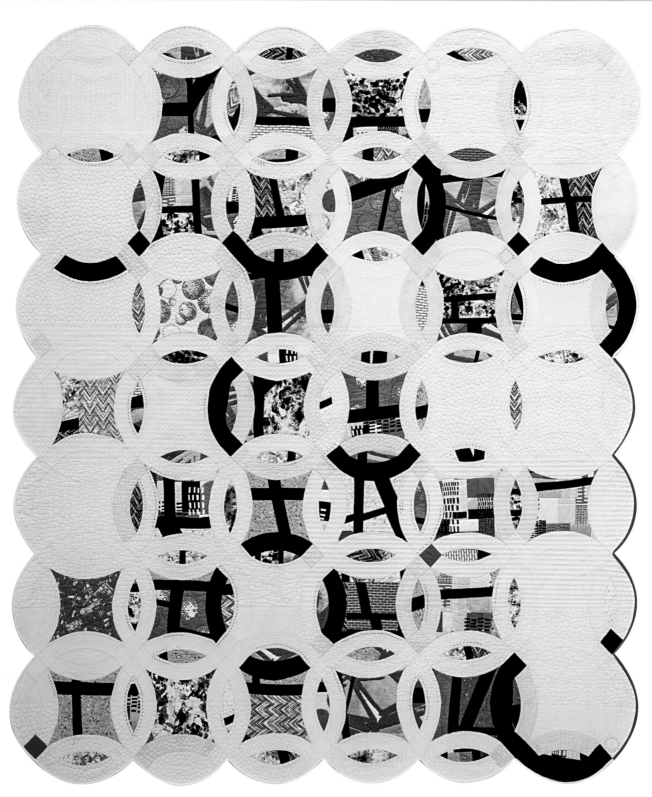

Double-Edged Love by Victoria Findlay Wolfe, quilted by Lisa Sipes, 2013, 66″ × 77″

FABRIC REQUIREMENTS

- **Made-Fabric** (page 108)**:** 16 fat quarters for background squares and melons
- **Muslin:** 6 yards for various pieces and binding
- **Black:** 1½ yards for arcs, squares, and slashing
- **Light pink:** 1¼ yards for arcs and squares
- **Red:** ⅝ yard for partial binding and 2 squares
- **Lavender:** Scrap for 1 arc
- **Backing:** 5 yards
- **Batting:** 76″ × 87″

Preparing Slashed Fabric

Slash and insert black strips into Made-Fabric fat quarters (page 109).

CUTTING

Arcs
- Cut 194 arcs from muslin, black, pink, and lavender fabrics, using the AccuQuilt arc pattern (pullout page P1).

Squares
- Cut 194 squares from muslin, black, pink, and red fabrics, using the AccuQuilt small square pattern (pullout page P1).

Melons
- Cut 97 melons from muslin and Made-Fabric, using the AccuQuilt small melon pattern (pullout page P1).

Background squares
- Cut 42 background squares from muslin and Made-Fabric, using the AccuQuilt background pattern (pullout page P1).

Binding
- Cut a 32″ square from muslin and an 18″ square from red.

Piecing

Piece the quilt according to Basic Double Wedding Ring Construction (page 102). Make a total of 97 pieced melons.

Quilt Construction

1. Construct the quilt according to Basic Double Wedding Ring Construction (page 102).

2. Make approximately 280″ of 2½″ bias binding from the muslin square and 42″ of 2½″ bias binding from the red square, for a total of 322″ of bias binding. Refer to the quilt photo (page 16) to piece binding and add to quilt edges.

3. Quilt and bind.

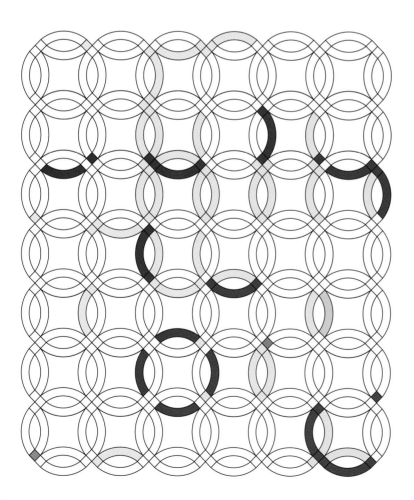

You Are
HERE

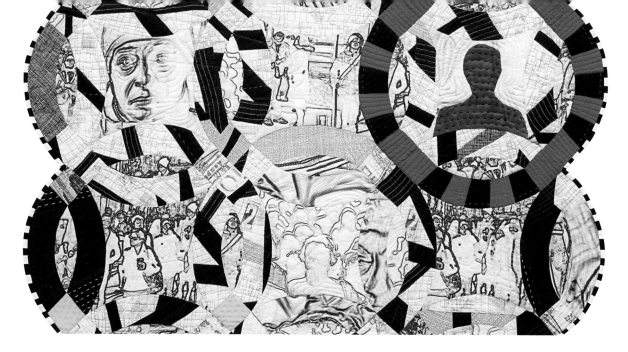

One of my main focuses when I make a quilt is to always find something I have not done before. When I went to visit the Brooklyn Museum's quilt exhibit and saw the dedication quote from Patricia Mainardi's *Quilts: The Great American Art* (1978) on the wall, "For all women everywhere, who never really wanted to be anonymous after all," I thought about how it related well to where I am now, living in New York City. This is the place where people say, "If you can make it here, you can make it anywhere."

Trying something you have never done before opens up a palette of life experiences that can start to appear.

I arrived in New York City in November 1994 with $200 in my pocket. I had a suitcase, a box of paintings, and a thin winter coat. I knew no one. I felt like a lost seed blown away from the pod, looking to see where life would lead me. Anonymous and a bit lost and homeless, I had everything stolen from me, and suddenly I felt like I had the spotlight on me in a way I did not want. My paintings were now gone, I had a bag of clothes, and I was homeless for two months. I was faced with either finding a real job or going back to Minnesota.

That city-street experience felt like it might be a great healing journey to share in this small quilt. And some elements and ideas from making *Double-Edged Love* (page 12) still needed to be explored further. I wanted to focus on making my own printed fabric through photographs to tell the story and add in as many other techniques as I could to make a very "new-to-me" kind of quilt.

IDEAS CARRIED OVER
from *Double-Edged Love* (page 12)

▸ New York City street views

▸ Slashing

THE GOAL

▸ Use images of NYC.

▸ Consider how *anonymous* fits.

▸ Add many techniques together: sashing, hand and machine quilting, overprinting.

Focusing on elements from *Double-Edged Love* inspired ideas to apply to this quilt.

I stripped the color out of some photographs using Photoshop and printed them on fabric. When you are alone in a big city, things tend to be pretty black and white—stripped down, as I was, without all my belongings. But glimmers of color popped into my world here and there. Coming to New York City was my way of getting a clean slate. It started white, and color began to creep into my painting of life, to find who I am. . . .

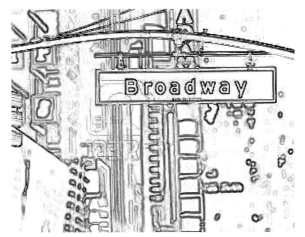

Take a photo. Use Photoshop filters to strip away the color, and then print it on fabric.

ADD LAYERS

Once I had the fabric designs created, I printed some on my home printer and had Spoonflower (spoonflower.com) print the others. I also used my Tsukineko inks to add information on top of the images where it was needed. Mind you, this was way out of my comfort zone. Trying something you have never done before not only opens up that field of knowledge and fear of not knowing, but also opens up a palette of life experiences that can start to appear.

PUSH IT FURTHER

▶ How can I add hand and machine quilting to tell the story?

▶ How could I show how I felt in those early New York City days?

▶ How could I convey how I feel now . . . the streets, the mass chaos of people?

▶ What colors first marked my senses?

▶ How could I capture that alone, singled-out feeling?

▶ I used the red heart from the "I heart NYC" logo and the yellow, representing the taxis and street markings.

▶ Stitching together areas in the quilt felt like how I started to build my community of people around me, how I was building a comfortable surrounding in my life and not just in what I was quilting.

All of this is what goes into a quilt when I start with nothing . . . and turn it into something.

You Are Here by Victoria Findlay Wolfe, 2012, 37¾″ × 48″

Double Wedding Ring Quilts—Traditions Made Modern

FABRIC REQUIREMENTS

- **Slashed Made-Fabric** (page 108): 8 fat quarters for arcs, squares, and melons

- **Printed fabric:** 1¾ yards for arcs, squares, background, melons, and background squares

- **Black:** ¾ yard for arcs, arc wedges, squares, and slashing

- **Light red print:** ¼ yard for arc and melon

- **Yellow:** ⅛ yard for squares

- **Solid red:** ¼ yard for arc wedges and squares

- **Binding:** ¾ yard of striped fabric

- **Backing:** 2¾ yards

- **Batting:** 48″ × 58″

TIP *To figure the shape of the top right corner, sew 3 pieced melons to a background square. Press and use as a template to cut the larger shape as a whole. Template plastic is great to have on hand in the studio.*

CUTTING

Arcs

- Cut 52 arcs from Made-Fabric, printed fabric, and black and light red print fabrics, using the AccuQuilt arc pattern (pullout page P1).

- Cut 4 each black wedges 1, 3, and 5 and 4 each red wedges 2 and 4, using You Are Here wedge patterns (pullout page P1).

Squares

- Cut 56 squares from Made-Fabric, printed fabric, and yellow and solid red fabrics, using the AccuQuilt small square pattern (pullout page P1).

Melons

- Cut 28 melons from Made-Fabric, printed fabric, and light red fabric, using the AccuQuilt small melon pattern (pullout page P1).

Background squares

- Cut 11 background squares from printed fabric, using the AccuQuilt background pattern (pullout page P1).

Top right corner

- Cut shape per Tip (at left).

Binding

- Cut 6 strips 2½″ × width of fabric from striped fabric, or make 185″ of bias binding.

Piecing

Piece the quilt according to Basic Double Wedding Ring Construction (page 102). Make 4 pieced arcs and a total of 28 pieced melons.

Quilt Construction

1. Construct the quilt according to Basic Double Wedding Ring Construction (page 102).

2. Quilt and bind.

Greatest Possible
TRUST

Donna Mae's Crazy Quilt, Elda Wolfe,
1990, 70″ × 81″

This quilt, made by my grandmother, was the inspiration quilt for *Greatest Possible Trust*. Elda's style and color palette have definitely influenced my own work.

When I was asked to submit a quilt to the New England Quilt Museum's *Modern* exhibition and to include one of my grandmother's quilts in the exhibit, I had a pretty good idea right away how to represent both traditionalism and modernism, because *Double-Edged Love* (page 12) had defined *modern* for me. I wanted to make another quilt showing how I had learned to quilt, inspired by my grandmother's work, and how the two blend together.

> *Her colors, patterns, and designs affected my own natural color palette.*

I learned the appreciation of quilts by sleeping under my grandmother Elda Wolfe's abstract crazy polyester quilts. Her colors, patterns, and designs affected my own natural color palette. Grandma's piecing obviously influenced how I work improvisationally. I wanted to take my approach, include her traditional style, and take the fresh concept of using white in modern quilts, mixing it together like paint to make a collaboration quilt of that knowledge. Blending her style with mine, I let them collide with great force.

I focused on the color red; it often appears as the strongest color in both my grandmother's quilts and mine. I played with negative space in a more traditional Double Wedding Ring sense as well as using red in a modern way, letting the two styles bleed together—her vintage 1960–1970s cotton scraps in her scrappy made-fabric way and my Made-Fabric (see Basic Made-Fabric and Slashing Techniques, page 108) to signify the era.

I was able to combine embroidery in the traditional quilting parts of the quilt and appliqué in the modern portion in red. My grandmother was quite proficient in handwork, and I wanted to include as much of her as I could in this quilt.

I had a great time deciding how many "new" elements I could add to this quilt: What could I add to the Double Wedding Ring design? How do I add interest to the binding, the edge of the quilt, and the quilting?

I try to add hand and machine work to every quilt I make. It adds to the traditional and modern aspects of my work. I added a floral quilting motif through the top half of the quilt. I also added modern, straight-line quilting to the bottom half, while adding some traditional appliqué into those areas to make them stand out. As a modern twist, I added embroidery over the quilting lines only where they crossed into the red sections of the quilt.

I added the extra red squares in the setting concave arcs at the quilt's edge to change it slightly from the white top half of the quilt. Last, I played up the binding so that the color would match the color it is touching in the quilt—white on white, red on red, or blending it where it needed to. All these details and elements help tell the story and make a complete thought.

Greatest Possible Trust. Why this name? Family. My happiest childhood memories are driving the four hours to get to Grandma's house, walking in the porch door, having the delicious aroma of Grandma's house hit me as I walked into the kitchen, and finding a gallon ice-cream bucket filled with my favorite sugar cookies made just for me. Life there was so different from life on the farm I grew up on. When you are a kid, you view the grown-ups around you through a magnifying glass. I trusted that these people would always be good to me. I felt the love when I walked through their door. They held the "greatest possible trust" about what family meant to me.

IDEAS CARRIED OVER
from *You Are Here* (page 19)

▸ Minnesota to New York City

▸ Modern and traditional

THE GOAL

▸ Incorporate what I do with how I learned to quilt from my grandmother—a collaboration of the two styles coming together.

ADD LAYERS

▸ Use new and vintage fabrics from the '70s.

▸ Mix modern and traditional quilting.

▸ Add handwork, embroidery, and appliqué.

PUSH IT FURTHER

▸ Think about your edges; change the pattern by looking at the final overall shape.

▸ How else can you make the distinction between modern and traditional?

▸ Don't forget your binding and backing choices; make it a complete story.

TIP *Prewash vintage fabrics!*

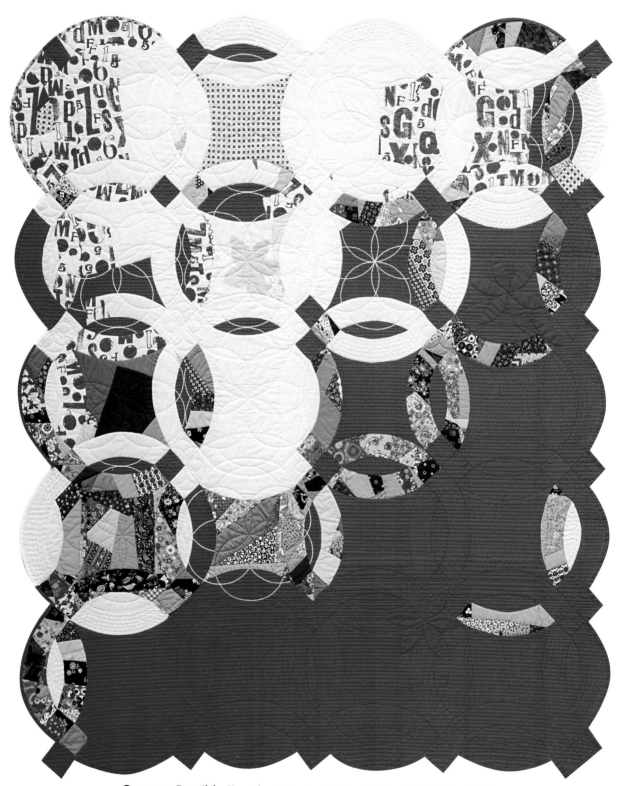

Greatest Possible Trust by Victoria Findlay Wolfe, 2013, 47˝ × 57½˝

Double Wedding Ring Quilts—Traditions Made Modern

FABRIC REQUIREMENTS

- **Made-Fabric** (page 108)**:** 8 fat quarters for arcs, squares, melons, and background squares

- **Red:** 3¼ yards for arcs, squares, melons, background squares, binding, and appliqué

- **White:** 1⅞ yards for arcs, squares, melons, background squares, and binding

- **Red-and-white prints:** 1½ yards total for arcs, squares, melons, background squares, Made-Fabric, and binding

- **Backing:** 3¼ yards

- **Batting:** 57″ × 68″

CUTTING

Arcs
- Cut 98 arcs from red, white, print, and Made-Fabrics, using the AccuQuilt arc pattern (pullout page P1).

Squares
- Cut 109 squares from red, white, print, and Made-Fabrics, using the AccuQuilt small square pattern (pullout page P1).

Melons
- Cut 49 melons from red, white, print, and Made-Fabrics, using the AccuQuilt small melon pattern (pullout page P1).

Background squares
- Cut 20 background squares from print, white, red, and Made-Fabrics, using the AccuQuilt background pattern (pullout page P1).

Appliqué
- Cut 12 flower petals, using the petal pattern and adding a seam allowance if needed. Appliqué as desired.

Binding
- Cut 8 strips 2½″ × width of fabric from a combination of red, white, and print fabrics, or make 274″ of bias binding.

Piecing

Piece the quilt according to Basic Double Wedding Ring Construction (page 102). Make a total of 49 pieced melons.

Quilt Construction

1. Construct the quilt according to Basic Double Wedding Ring Construction (page 102).

2. Quilt and bind.

3. Add appliqué flower petals as desired.

NOTE

To distinguish the two styles, add extra red squares on the bottom and right outside edges when constructing the rows.

Bright Lights,
BIG CITY

Finding my path in New York City has always been an adventure. From the moment I got there, I thought, *I need to change the way I think about people, life, and experiences… I need to keep all my options open to see where life wants to lead me.*

Funny enough, when I think about how I approach quilt-making, it's exactly the same thing. Keep all the options open; let ideas, memories, colors, and tools collide and let them all explode on the design wall.

Four months after arriving in the city, a man walked into my job at a frame shop. I helped him and went about my day. The next day, I was off work. The man came back and left a note and two tickets for me to attend an art opening. I thought, Oh, that was so nice of him! But I had no idea what that meant. Was he just being nice or did this mean something?

Keep all the options open; let ideas, memories, colors, and tools collide and let them all explode on the design wall.

Who do I take with me? Do I bring a date? Do I bring my co-worker? Do I go by myself? Should I go at all? I was still a newbie to the city and that idea of keeping all my options open meant I was going to experience an art opening, since I had never been to one.

So I went!

Fast-forward four years: That man and I wed, started plans for a family, and found a place that would be our home. The Double Wedding Ring signifies both my marriage and the winding path of my life, to that very day.

We found a loft home in the heart of the garment center and just four blocks from Times Square. We are truly in the heart of the city. At the time we moved to this area, it was filled with peep shows and garment-sewing sweat shops by day, and was deserted by 5 p.m. Shortly after we

Double Wedding Ring Quilts—Traditions Made Modern

moved in, the Times Square revitalization hit, and the neighborhood changed almost overnight. We lived in the only residential building on our block at the time, and there were many empty lots and parking facilities. Before the market crashed, everything sold, buildings went up, garment sewing was moved out of the city, and now everyone wants to live where we do—funny how things change.

All that history went into this quilt. I envisioned a fatter, more robust Double Wedding Ring pattern to be able to add in bits of the New York Beauty style into my New York City quilt. Adding the glow of the city, by using my favorite color of orange, the neon lights, the flicker of electricity, the people, the chaos, and even a few cowgirls. It's flavor, no doubt, the twinkling of the Big Apple, a trail of that energy, that has led to happiness—I love raising my daughter in a big, open New York City loft.

Using about 150 different fabrics to make this scrappy beauty was so much fun. My fabric selections were purely based on whether I loved the fabric—including *orange*, my favorite color!

IDEAS CARRIED OVER
from *You Are Here* (page 19)

▶ New York City feelings from *You Are Here* to where I am now

▶ A new view on New York City

▶ Scrappy traditional quality with modern and vintage fabrics

THE GOAL

▶ Develop a new pattern for the Double Wedding Ring.

▶ Work with my favorite color—orange.

ADD LAYERS

▶ Select a massive number of fabrics (about 150 fabrics were used) and make them live harmoniously together and show my *joy*!

PUSH IT FURTHER

▶ Use novelty fabrics to help tell the story.

▶ Can you change the pattern in one more way with fabric placement?

▶ Can you modify the New York Beauty unit in some, but not all, of the blocks?

▶ How does the style and pattern change through color placement?

▶ Can you change one more element in the pattern to tell your story?

▶ Can you create your own paper-pieced design to work inside any of the templates?

▶ Can you look at your light and dark fabrics and play on the twinkling effect?

Bright Lights, Big City by Victoria Findlay Wolfe, quilted by Shelly Pagliai, 2013, 90˝ × 90˝

Double Wedding Ring Quilts—Traditions Made Modern

FABRIC REQUIREMENTS

The beauty of this quilt is its large-scale scrappiness— the fabric suggestions are only estimates.

- **Mostly orange-tone fabrics:** 15 yards of mostly ½-yard cuts

- **Orange print:** 1 yard for binding

- **Backing:** 8⅜ yards

- **Batting:** 100″ × 100″

CUTTING

Arcs
- Cut 288 background pieces and 216 spikes for the paper-pieced spiked arcs using Bright Lights, Big City arc pattern A (pullout page P2).

Squares
- Cut 72 squares 6½″ × 6½″ or using Bright Lights, Big City square pattern B (pullout page P1).

Melons
- Cut 36 melons using Bright Lights, Big City small melon pattern C (pullout page P2).

Center diamond
- Cut 13 center diamonds and 8 side setting diamonds using Bright Lights, Big City center diamond and side setting diamond patterns D and E (pullout page P1).

Binding
- Cut 10 strips 2½″ × width of fabric from orange print, or make 340″ of bias binding.

Paper-Pieced Arcs

The paper-pieced arcs must go together before you can sew anything else.

1. Make 72 copies of Bright Lights, Big City arc pattern A (pullout page P2).

2. Piece the arcs using the pattern and Basic Paper Piecing (page 110). Make 72 arcs.

3. Trim them to the edge of the pattern.

NOTE

There is no prescribed order for color/print placement; just look for good contrast between the triangle points and the background of each arc. For added design interest, I also fussy cut some of the larger novelty prints into the larger portions of a few arcs.

Melon Blocks

Using the paper-pieced arcs, small melons, and squares, stitch the melon blocks according to Basic Double Wedding Ring Construction (page 102). Make a total of 36 melon blocks.

Quilt Construction

1. Construct the quilt according to Basic Double Wedding Ring Construction (page 102).

2. Quilt and bind.

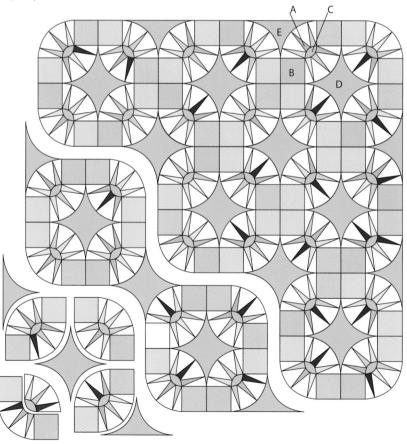

Retro
POLY MOD

Ahhh, those s t r e t c h y fabrics. What fond memories we all have of them. Fond? Okay, stop laughing! We all wore them! Yes, I am old enough to have worn matching polyester stretchy outfits with my mom, brother, and even my grandpa and cousins … proof!

Grandpa Leo with my brother, cousins, and me, all in matching polyester double-knit shirts, made by my mother!

Growing up on a farm, in a house heated with wood stoves, certainly makes one very happy to have a heavy, double-knit polyester quilt with two layers of polyester batting encased inside and tied! You didn't actually move much under them! They stayed nicely in place, while you shimmied into your clothes under the covers in the cold of the early morning. Once the stoves were lit again and the house began to warm, then you were good to go. Just do not get near a flame!

I have been collecting double-knit fabrics for a while now, waiting for just the right project. If I have come this far and base everything I do

on where I came from, then how could I not make a polyester quilt?

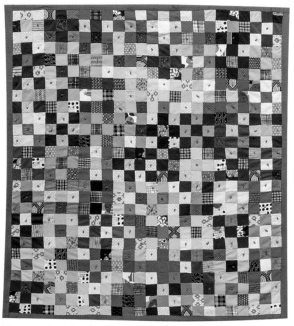

My grandmother had a very definite color palette that consistently appears in her work. I think that palette has heavily influenced my own work.

The colors of my grandmother's quilts are what got me through sleepless bedtimes. It would take me hours to fall asleep as a kid because I could not turn off my brain. I was always thinking creative thoughts! I've learned now to meditate and calm myself, but as a kid, tracing the colors of Grandma's quilts, looking for my favorite print, and meandering through the maze of her patchwork would get me to quiet myself and eventually fall asleep. In addition to the weight of those quilts, there is something very comforting about having that heaviness holding you in place and comforting you.

I have been collecting polyester quilts too, mostly out of nostalgia, but also because each one makes me think of Grandma. I cannot leave a quilt unloved in a thrift store

or antique shop, so my collection has grown quite rapidly. It is not just the quilts but those bright-colored fabrics, so I figured now is as good a time as any to make that quilt.

What do I love most about a fabric that will be around forever?

First, the colors are spectacular! They will never fade. The yardage I have collected looks as good now as it did in 1970! I wish now that I had some of Grandma's old clothes to cut up and use in this quilt.

Second reason—I love the prints and what I've seen people do with polyester in quilts. From hand piecing to hand quilting, I think it is fantastic! I am amazed that people thought to make complicated patterns using this fabric. I searched for four years to find a vintage polyester Wedding Ring quilt, and I am happy to say I finally found one. It is as crazy and wonderful as I had hoped it would be!

My mother told me that she had asked her mother to make her a Double Wedding Ring quilt. She seems to think that Grandma

started making one but was frustrated by the whole process and abandoned that idea—I wonder what happened to *that UFO (unfinished object)*!

When I look at the colors of these fabrics, they just scream *modern* to me. So, as I looked at the different Double Wedding Ring patterns I came up with, I decided to use the largest pieces I could, so that I could truly show them off. I figured that solids would be even better and would radiate the polyester passion! I also had a few polyester quilt tops that were in shabby condition, so I cut out sections from the old top to add it to my story. You can see the arcs where I used the Nine-Patch quilt to add a few interesting pieced details in this quilt.

> *When I look at the colors of these fabrics, they just scream* modern *to me.*

Funny enough, my daughter, who says that my quilts are not soft enough for her, said after I finished this quilt, "Oh, Mom, it's so soft! I love it!" Go figure. You may notice that I tied the quilt, used wool batting for the loft, and also turned the backing fabric to the front for the binding, just as my grandmother would have done on hers.

Also note that using double knits makes this pattern sew together like a dream. Curves are extremely easy on a fabric that gives and forgives.

I'd also like to thank a few of my friends who decided I should have a few polyester patchwork garments to go with my collection. They figured I'd be the only one to appreciate them. Ha-ha! Strangely, they are right!

IDEAS CARRIED OVER
from *Bright Lights, Big City* (page 32)

▶ Focus on the same template set. What other design can you make with it?

▶ Change one more detail in either the layout, the color, or even the kind of fabric you choose. How about linen, corduroy, shirtings, or polyester?

THE GOAL

▶ Use double-knit polyester and/or find fabrics that you might not normally use.

ADD LAYERS

▶ Simplify the pattern of *Bright Lights, Big City* (page 32) to make it feel more modern.

▶ Play with scale.

▶ How does the pattern change depending on how you crop and edit the design?

▶ Recycle fabrics or quilt tops you have.

PUSH IT FURTHER

▶ Keep it as "old skool" as possible. Ha-ha!

▶ Turn the backing to the front for binding, as I learned to do as a kid.

▶ Learn a new binding technique.

▶ Tie the quilt.

Retro Poly Mod by Victoria Findlay Wolfe, 2014, 60″ × 60″

Double Wedding Ring Quilts—Traditions Made Modern

FABRIC REQUIREMENTS

The beauty of this quilt is its large-scale scrappiness, so the fabric suggestions are only estimates. Polyester fabric yardage is based on 58˝ wide fabric.

- **Pink poly:** 1½ yards for center diamonds and side setting half-diamonds

- **Gold poly:** ¼ yard for melons

- **Poly scraps:** 32 squares 10˝ × 10˝ and 32 squares 6½˝ × 6½˝ for arcs and squares

- **Backing:** 4 yards of cotton fabric

- **Batting:** 70˝ × 70˝

- **Yarn:** For tying the quilt

- **Chenille needle:** Size 16

CUTTING

Arcs:
- Cut 32 arcs from 10˝ × 10˝ poly scraps, using Bright Lights, Big City arc pattern A (pullout page P2). (Ignore paper-piecing lines.)

NOTE

I started by cutting 1 arc and 1 square out of each poly scrap I had. Then I cut additional pieces, like extra red squares, to fill in as I played with the layout.

Squares:
- Cut 32 squares from 6½˝ × 6½˝ poly scraps or use Bright Lights, Big City square pattern B (pullout page P1).

Melons:
- Cut 16 melons from gold poly, using Bright Lights, Big City small melon pattern C (pullout page P2).

Diamonds:
- Cut 4 center diamonds and 8 side setting diamonds from pink poly, using Bright Lights, Big City center diamond and side setting diamond patterns D and E (pullout page P2).

Piecing

Piece the quilt according to Basic Double Wedding Ring Construction (page 102). Make a total of 16 pieced melons.

NOTE

Even though these melons are bigger and fatter than usual, they are sewn together the same way.

Quilt Construction

1. Construct the quilt according to Basic Double Wedding Ring Construction (page 102).

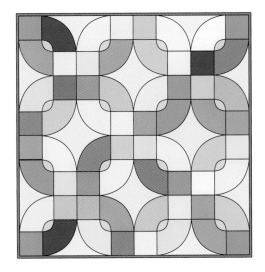

2. Tie the quilt by taking a stitch and tying a knot in the yarn. Refer to the quilt photo (previous page) for knot placement.

3. Fold the backing over to the front and hand stitch to finish the edge.

Strings of Florid
BLOOMS

Double Wedding Ring Quilts—Traditions Made Modern

This quilt uses the same pattern as *Bright Lights, Big City* (page 32) (minus paper piecing the arcs) and *Retro Poly Mod* (page 39). Three quilts from one pattern! This just excites me to no end, and I have several more in my head. Having the larger template pieces allows you to add more piecing inside of each piece, or *not*. On this quilt, I wanted to make a great, white, modern-looking quilt that shows off a fantastic color palette and highlights the negative space. I made *one* change to the pattern—I added ash squares in the middle of some of the white blocks. Each white block alone is 6½˝, which works really nicely if you have other patterns for 6½˝ blocks! What else could you drop in there?

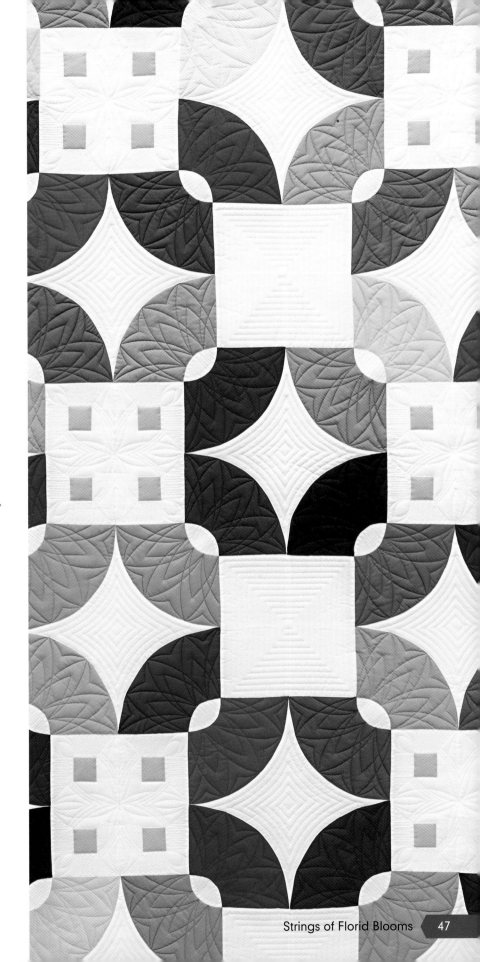

Strings of Florid Blooms by Victoria Findlay Wolfe, quilted by Shelly Pagliai, 2014, 90˝ × 90˝

Double Wedding Ring Quilts—Traditions Made Modern

FABRIC REQUIREMENTS

- **White:** 6¼ yards for center diamonds and side setting diamonds, melons, squares, and pieced squares.

- **Ash:** ⅓ yard for small squares

- **Kona fat quarters:** Clover, Willow, Palm, Peapod, Leprechaun, Aloe, Sunflower, Robin Egg, Alegria, Cyan, Ocean, Tulip, Thistle, Pansy, Lavender, Cerise, Poppy, Azalea, Candy Pink, Plum, Peony, Blush Pink, Melon, and Nautical for arcs

- **Binding:** ⅞ yard of Kona Alegria

- **Backing:** 8½ yards

- **Batting:** 100″ × 100″

TIP *There are great apps on smart phones for adapting quilt blocks to any size. Your options to drop another design into each 6½″ block are endless!*

CUTTING

Arcs:

- Cut 72 arcs from assorted Kona colors, using Bright Lights, Big City arc pattern A (pullout page P2). (Ignore paper-piecing lines.) I cut 3 from each fat quarter.

Squares:

- Cut 36 squares from white 6½″ × 6½″ or use Bright Lights, Big City square pattern B (pullout page P1).

Pieced squares:

- Cut 36 squares 2½″ × 2½″ from ash. Cut 72 squares 2½″ × 2½″ from white. Cut 72 rectangles 2½″ × 6½″ from white.

Melons:

- Cut 36 melons from white, using Bright Lights, Big City small melon pattern C (pullout page P2).

Background squares:

- Cut 12 center diamonds and 12 side setting diamonds from white, using Bright Lights, Big City center diamond pattern D and side setting diamond E (pullout page P2).

Binding:

- Cut 10 strips 2½″ × width of fabric from the binding fabric.

NOTE

Depending on how you lay out your colors, you can make a variety of patterns with this design. If you are a *15 Minutes of Play* "Made-Fabric queen" like me, you might consider dropping in Made-Fabric (see Basic Made-Fabric and Slashing Techniques, page 108) into those big arcs! Yes, I may be making that quilt, too. What about taking your orphan blocks or orphan quilt top and cutting them out using the patterns?

Piecing

The pieced squares must go together before you can sew anything else.

PIECED SQUARES

1. Sew an ash 2½˝ × 2½˝ square between 2 white 2½˝ × 2½˝ squares.

2. Sew that pieced unit between 2 rectangles 2½˝ × 6½˝. Make 36 pieced squares.

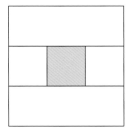

MELONS

Using the pieced squares, stitch the pieced melons according to Basic Double Wedding Ring Construction (page 102). Make a total of 36 pieced melons using 1 white square and 1 pieced square per melon.

Quilt Construction

1. Construct the quilt according to Basic Double Wedding Ring Construction (page 102).

2. Quilt and bind.

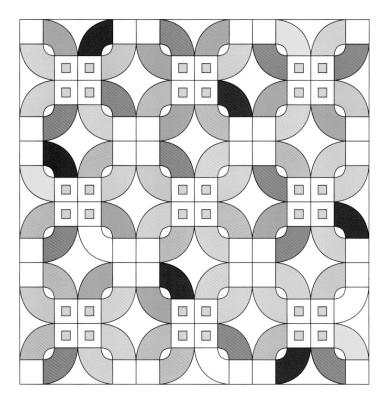

LEONA

Leona was inspired by a vintage quilt top, affectionately called *Olga* (below right). In honor of my grandfather Leo and his twin sister, Leona, I designed this quilt to play on the color memories of the family photo and just how opposite they were as twins!

Olga, Double Wedding Ring variation vintage top, owned by Edie McGinnis, Kansas City, Missouri, possibly made in Iowa

When I started this series, I drew some basic ideas on paper of what I wanted to achieve. This is *not* the way I normally work. I do not like knowing ahead of time what a quilt will look like in the end. I prefer those discoveries to happen on their own, keeping all my options open. I do not want to shut down my creativity because I have a predetermined set path. But on this quilt, I drew a design that had an odd pattern that somewhat resembled the old cash register receipt tape, pulled from a register and the ink smeared. It was something I remembered— running through the alley as a kid from my grandparents' house to the Kwik Trip to buy candy, such as raspberry bubble gum, Laffy Taffy, and Pixy Stix.

Donna Mae's Crazy Quilt, Elda Wolfe, 1990, 70″ × 81″

Once I saw *Olga*, my memories and creative play started to make connections, and all the ideas fell into place. The colors in the photo of Leo and Leona were inspiring! I dug through my stash and found about 30 antique Double Wedding Ring melons I had bought on eBay. They were made of shirtings and plaids that made me think of my grandfather Leo's work shirts. I thought about how Grandma saved everything and cut things up to make them into something else. I thought, *Okay, what can I do with these to give them new life?*

I do not want to shut down my creativity because I have a predetermined set path.

Double-Knit Red, White, and Blue, Elda Wolfe, 1983, 74″ × 79″

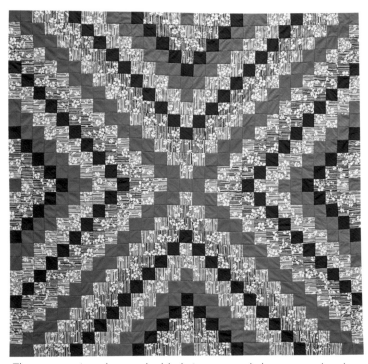

These two twin polyester double-knit tops, made by my grandmother Elda Wolfe, are definitely part of the family "twin" tradition!

Grandpa's day job was working at the Big Jo Flour Mill, which had a big red, white, and blue logo. I tend to associate colors with people, so when I think of him, I think red, and bottle green for his car, and navy blue for his work trousers. This gave me my natural color palette to start to play with.

As I cut apart the not-so-nicely-sewn-together Double Wedding Rings of days gone by, I was drawn to the plaids of green and gold that were showing up with red and blue. I realized that the earlier idea that I had drawn initially was happening all by itself in this new design. The pattern repeats, then changes, then picks back up again. Where *Olga* had issues, the new drawn pattern went together like butter. I now had this quilt that felt like my grandfather Leo.

IDEAS CARRIED OVER
from *Bright Lights, Big City* (page 32)

▸ Dissect the pattern even more.

▸ Play on color, pattern, and personal memories.

THE GOAL

▸ Influenced by *Olga* (page 52), the design and construction flaws were my challenge idea. Incorporate twins, twin quilts, twins in the family.

▸ Use old orphan blocks.

ADD LAYERS

▸ Use vintage melons and updated color palette; adapt them to fit the new design.

▸ Repurpose; be resourceful!

PUSH IT FURTHER

▸ Focus on deconstructing the pattern.

▸ What elements can you select and transform?

▸ Learn a new free-motion quilting design!

▸ Design a new pattern template.

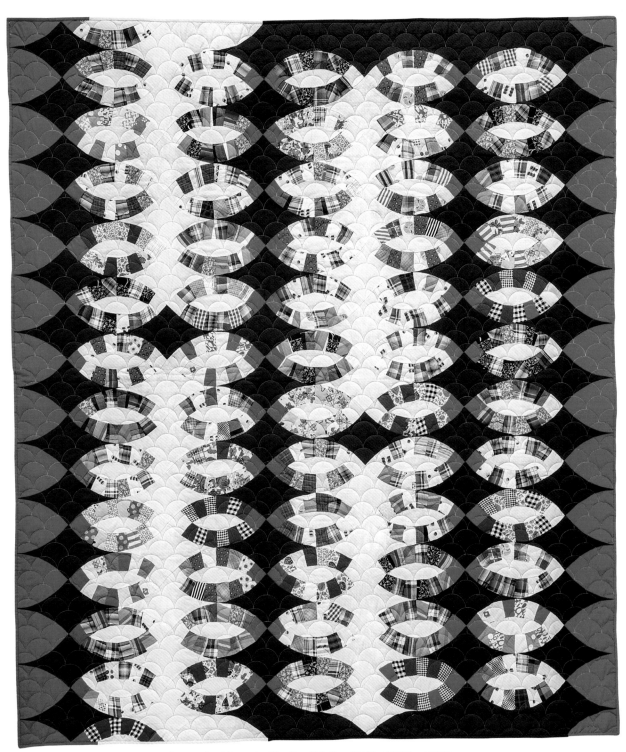

Leona by Victoria Findlay Wolfe, 2013, 69½˝ × 78½˝

Double Wedding Ring Quilts—Traditions Made Modern

FABRIC REQUIREMENTS

- **Plaids and prints:** Assorted pieces and scraps to total 3 yards for arc wedges

- **Red:** 1¾ yards for squares, edge melons, corner melons, and binding

- **White:** 3½ yards for squares, center melons, edge melons, background pieces, and binding

- **Indigo:** 4¼ yards for edge melons, background pieces, background, and binding

- **Backing:** 5 yards

- **Batting:** 80″ × 89″

CUTTING

Arc wedges:
- Cut 732 arc wedges from assorted prints and plaids using the Leona arc wedge F pattern (pullout page P2).

Squares:
- Cut 62 red and 62 white squares, using the Leona corner square G pattern (pullout page P2).

Center melons:
- Cut 62 center melons from white fabric using the Leona center melon H pattern (pullout page P2).

Edge melons:
- Cut 24 side melons from red fabric using the Leona side melon I pattern (pullout page P2). Cut 6 top/bottom melons from indigo fabric and 2 from white fabric using the Leona top/bottom melon J pattern (pullout page P2).

Corner melons:
- Cut 4 corner melons from red fabric using the Leona corner melon K pattern (pullout page P2).

Background:
- Cut 55 background pieces from indigo fabric and 23 from white fabric using the Leona background L pattern (pullout page P2).

Binding:
- Cut 5 strips 2½″ × width of fabric from red fabric, 1 strip 2½″ × width of fabric from white fabric, and 2 strips 2½″ × width of fabric from indigo fabric.

Piecing

Piece the melons according to Basic Double Wedding Ring Construction (page 102). Make a total of 62 pieced melons (2 will have only a single pieced arc and will be trimmed in half during construction).

Quilt Construction

This quilt's layout is different from traditional Double Wedding Ring quilts, and it has an equally unique approach to construction. In the end, though, it will go together using the same long, S-shaped, curvy seams as the others.

In all the other quilts, the background squares are pieced to the melons by pinning at the halfway points and matching the ends to prepare to sew the curved seam. In *Leona*, the background square reaches only halfway across the melon.

1. Pin a wide-point end of the background square to the end of the melon, and pin the narrow end of the background square to the center of the melon, matching the ¼˝ seam allowance of the background square to the center seam of the melon. Stitch it as if you were stitching the first half of the longer seams. Stop sewing at the center of the melon and backstitch. Fold the little seam allowance back. Press toward the background squares. Repeat until all the background squares have been stitched to a pieced melon.

NOTE

To easily create the long rows of background squares and melons, choose one quadrant of the melon to which you'll consistently add the background square, such as the upper left or the lower right.

2. Refer to the layout diagram (below) as you create the diagonal rows, being mindful of the color of the background squares as you go.

3. You'll need to add side melons to the end of each row; choose the correct shape by referring to the layout diagram. In the corners, use corner melons. In 2 places (top left and bottom center), you'll use pieced melons instead of top/bottom melons.

4. Sew the rows together. Match the center seams of the pieced melons to each other, and take care that the little folded-back seam allowances at the ends of the background squares meet.

5. When the top is complete, carefully trim the 2 pieced melons to align with the edges.

6. Quilt and bind.

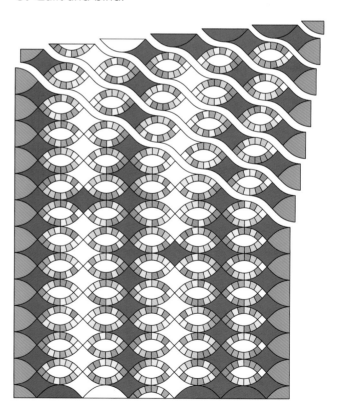

A Summer's
DAY

My grandparents had a massive garden. In addition to all the vegetables, Grandma had her side of the garden, which was filled with beds of peonies, and Grandpa had his, with irises and gladiolas. They grew and canned everything and stored it in the scary old dirt cellar full of spiders that I hated going to fetch things from.

Grandma always was taking slips of plants and had many pots of starter flowers next to her rocking chair in the house. When my grandmother was moved from her house to my aunt's, and the house was sold, I asked if I might have some of the peony, iris, and gladiola plants from their garden for my house on Long Island. I can happily say that those flowers still bloom here in New York, and I think of my grandparents every time I see them.

A couple summers ago, I visited my cousin Dale and asked if I could see Grandma's quilts that he had. He had quite a stack of them sitting on a window seat at the top of the stairs. The stack was rather large, mostly because she would put two layers of polyester batting inside each quilt, so that they felt like bricks on top of you, and of course kept you very warm during those Minnesota winters! As we were looking at them, he pulled out a quilt that belonged to my late cousin, Darron. As it fell open, I had a very faint memory of her working on this quilt, but I had not seen it in a very, very long time. My breath was taken away! This is a true work of art! See *Elda's Double-Knit Flowers* (bottom left).

Elda's Double-Knit Flowers, Elda Wolfe, circa 1985, 65″ × 80″

I added a Made-Fabric inner border, squared it up, included appliqué elements that related to the style of the quilt, and added Double Wedding Rings to make it into a medallion quilt. Lastly, I constructed the pieced Made-Fabric border, incorporating a flower design in the lower right, inspired by my grandmother's quilt.

When I think of how my grandmother pieced a few pieces at a time, on a sheet stretched out in front of her on a card table, and how she worked this out so beautifully, it tells me how talented she was. No design walls, making things up as she went along, and this great flower bursting through the scraps and peeking out in the corners as if it was a part of a larger quilt design—I was in awe.

This design spoke to me right away, and I had to think of how I could interpret that concept into my own version.

I had been playing around with an idea of using an orphan star block, only to realize I had not done a great job at constructing it. However, that never stops me from making a beautiful quilt. I always meet the challenge of how I can work with the mistake and turn it into a beauty.

Why put away an old quilt top that isn't speaking to you when you could cut it up, add to it, and make it into the thing of beauty you had initially set about making in the first place?

A quilt top might not be perfect, so we put it away. Eventually, many of these end up in thrift shops unfinished, until someone like me comes along, buys them, and attempts to breathe new life into them.

Cut those tops up! Make them beautiful! What do you have to lose? You have more fabric; I know you do! Go for it!

This was a long work in progress. What started as a pretty unsuccessful 15 Minutes of Play block was cut apart and transformed into a thing of beauty when inspiration and imagination made the connection! My grandmother's flower quilt was the spark that set the new course.

THINK OUT OF YOUR BOX

▶ How can you fix it? Don't focus on the oopsie.

▶ Change your thinking! Is it sad and ugly? How can you update the color palette?

▶ How can you make the oopsie into a positive?

▶ What would change it?

▶ What can you add to make it fabulous?

▶ Can you cut it? Add to it? Appliqué? Embroider?

I loved the lime green and all the scrappy fabrics in my pieced-star block, so I cut the block apart at the seams and inserted 1″ strips of fabric to fix where the block had issues. After I trimmed it down, I had another oopsie moment. It was not straight, but I could see that this piece still had value.

The lime green, orange, red, and pink is a reference to my grandmother's double-knit polyester color palette. This is of course a tribute to my grandmother's work. She would never have given up and tossed a less-than-perfect block aside. Keep persevering until you find an answer. Play out all the options. You may surprise yourself!

IDEAS CARRIED OVER
from *Leona* (page 51)

▶ Use my own orphan block/top.

▶ Rework to make it work!

THE GOAL

▶ Make my own interpretation of *Elda's Double-Knit Flowers* (page 60).

▶ Fix a UFO block. Cut the original block apart to fix it and add a new element.

ADD LAYERS

▶ Make the quilt to sprout leaves.

▶ Add appliqué to make a more purposeful design intent.

▶ Use elements from Grandma's quilt in mine.

PUSH IT FURTHER

▶ Embrace your mistakes and make a beautiful quilt.

▶ Cut, shape, and turn an old quilt top into something beautiful.

▶ Look at the colors and see how you can brighten and bring the look up to date. What other element of the story can you add to the quilt?

*A **Summer's Day*** by Victoria Findlay Wolfe, quilted by Debby Ritenbaugh Brown, 2010–2014, 67½˝ × 67½˝

FABRIC REQUIREMENTS

- **Orange:** 1¾ yards for arcs, squares, slashing, and appliqué
- **Lime green:** 1⅛ yards for background and melons
- **Bright yellow:** ½ yard for bias flange
- **Assorted fabrics:** Pieces from scraps up to fat eighths to total 3 yards of Made-Fabric
- **UFO block:** 16″–18″ square
- **Neon pink:** ¾ yard for binding
- **Backing:** 4½ yards
- **Batting:** 78″ × 78″

CUTTING

Arcs:
- Cut 48 arcs from orange fabric, using the AccuQuilt arc pattern (pullout page P1).

Squares:
- Cut 48 squares from orange fabric, using the AccuQuilt small square pattern (pullout page P1).

Melons:
- Cut 24 melons from lime green fabric, using the AccuQuilt small melon pattern (pullout page P1).

Background squares:
- Cut 4 background squares from lime green fabric, using the AccuQuilt background pattern (pullout page P1).
- Cut 8 half-background squares from lime green fabric, using one-half of the AccuQuilt background pattern (pullout page P1). Fold the full pattern in half diagonally and then add a ¼″ seam allowance to the folded side.

Slashing and appliqué:
- Cut 3 strips 1″ × width of fabric; 24 leaf shapes from orange fabric, using the leaf pattern; and 1 circle, using the center circle pattern. Cut 4 small circles from yellow scraps, using the small circle pattern (pullout page P2).

Flange trim:
- Cut 9 bias strips ¾″ wide for a total of 6 yards from bright yellow.

Binding:
- Cut 8 strips 2½″ × width of fabric from neon pink.

Piecing

ORPHAN BLOCK

1. Use a block you've saved or create a center block with a finished size of 16″–18″ square.

2. Cut the block in half and insert a 1″ strip of orange (see Slashing Techniques, page 109).

3. Repeat Step 1, slicing another direction, 3 more times, creating the asterisk arrangement.

4. Add leaves to these strips, and add more leaves after the borders have been stitched on, so that they extend into the surrounding area. Add the center circle and then the 4 small circles at the corners.

TIP *I have used a star block, but you could adapt any orphan block to start your design. Look at your blocks and find an idea that you can base your own story on.*

MADE-FABRIC

1. Create Made-Fabric (page 108) to piece around the block.

You will need 2 strips as long as the sides of the UFO block and 2 strips as long as the sides of the UFO block with the Made-Fabric added. To determine the width of these strips, deduct the finished size of the block from 29½″, divide by 2, and then add seam allowances.

Example: If the finished size of your block is 18″, the finished width of the strips will be half of 11½″, or 5¾″. Add ½″ for seam allowances to this measurement.

2. Create Made-Fabric to piece around the Wedding Ring blocks.

You will need 2 strips 13″ × 43″ and 2 strips 13″ × 68″.

WEDDING RINGS

1. Follow Basic Double Wedding Ring Construction (page 102) to make pieced melons from the arcs, melons, and squares. Make a total of 24 pieced melons.

2. Arrange 4 pieced melons around a background square and stitch, creating a complete wedding ring.

3. Add a pieced melon to a half-background square.

4. Repeat Step 3 using a second pieced melon and half-background square to create a mirror image.

5. Place these pieced units on opposite sides of the pieced wedding ring with the flat edges of the half-background squares, creating a straight line along an edge. Make 4 units.

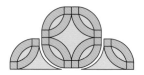

Quilt Construction

1. Stitch the 2 shortest narrow Made-Fabric strips onto opposite sides of the block. Press toward the block. Stitch the 2 longer narrow strips onto the remaining 2 sides. Press toward the block. Check the size of the resulting center medallion square. Trim, if necessary, to 30″ × 30″.

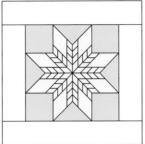

2. Stitch a wedding ring unit to a side of the central medallion. Repeat for all 4 sides of the medallion. Set aside.

3. Stitch the remaining 13″-wide Made-Fabric strips together to make a large square with a hole in the center. The wedding ring section will be appliquéd over the opening to the background. Set aside.

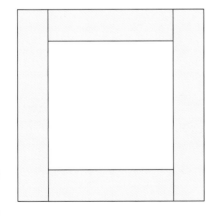

4. Piece the bias flange strips into a continuous strip. Press the strip lengthwise, wrong sides together and raw edges aligned.

5. Stitch the flange to the wedding ring section, right sides together, leaving a 1″ tail of the flange loose, and align the raw edge of the flange with the raw curved edge of the wedding ring section. Stitch in place. Overlap the ends once you've come all the way around. After stitching, roll the flange over so that the seam allowances roll to the wrong side of the wedding ring section and the flange extends ⅛″ from the edge. Clip the seam allowances at the inner corners so the piece lies flat. Press.

6. Carefully center the wedding ring section over the outer border of Made-Fabric. Match the centers of the border to the centers of the wedding ring section and pin or glue in place. Continue pinning or gluing around the edges, securing the curved edges in place. Appliqué in place by hand or machine, leaving the flange free.

NOTE

Appliqué glue is a great, fast way to adhere the top into place while it awaits stitching.

7. Quilt and bind.

LACE

Elda Wolfe's crocheted doily that inspired *Lace* (page 70)

My grandmother was prolific at crochet and embroidery. One of the things I recall the most as a kid is having a box of her doilies in the top cabinet in my room. Every once in a while, we'd take down the box, lift it open, and carefully leaf through her work, encouraging the doilies to lie as flat as they could, cajoling the ruffles to fall, hill and valley, as they may. My mother and I worked on an afghan together when I was young and learning to crochet, chaining shell after shell of cream, salmon, and brown variegated yarn. I never

I never felt I was a "doily person," but I have a huge appreciation for the skill.

thought I had the patience to actually make a whole blanket myself—I've started many and only finished one. My afghan UFOs and collection of yarn has grown almost as much as my fabric stash.

I never felt I was a "doily person," but I have a huge appreciation for the skill. Both my grandma and my aunt Judy were always making things that amazed me. Anytime we got to visit Grandma or Aunt Judy, there would always be a new crocheted toy for me—from dolls, donkeys, and clowns to Christmas stockings and blankets.

Lace by Victoria Findlay Wolfe, quilted by Lisa Sipes, 2014, 83˝ × 83˝

I still love to get out the box of doilies and admire them. A couple years ago, while visiting Aunt Judy, I walked in and, as always, she had something for me: two doilies made by Grandma. Each was made of the same cream thread crocheted in a lovely floral lace pattern, with a crimson red, delicate edge. As soon as I saw it, I had a vision of making a quilt that represented the work of these doilies. I gathered many lace print fabrics, five months before I even started designing the quilt. I knew it would be a complicated pattern. I had many thoughts about how I could develop and adapt the Double Wedding Ring pattern so all the arcs and scallops would give me the same feeling as holding the piece of lace work in my hands.

The parts department! Looking at my inspiration piece, I'm searching for elements that I can take and adapt into my quilt design. Here, I'm focused on how to incorporate the red scalloped edge into my quilt.

For me, working in white or light fabrics is a definite challenge. I love contrast. But here I wanted to focus on the subtle softness of the pattern and color to play out the delicate features of the crochet. I wanted to keep it as light as possible, but I was eager to find fabrics that would drop in a bit of subtle color here and there.

I started out making the five center blocks with the vintage red dainty floral fabrics (see the five pink flowers in the center of the quilt). I added strategically placed appliquéd petals in the center and around these five center blocks.

I knew I'd be adding that red detail edge to the border of the quilt. I also knew that I had to keep the scrappy nature to honor both Grandma's and my process. I was prepared for the long process of discovering the design in this quilt.

I was careful to scatter fabrics that had black, pink, and red among the blocks. Constantly looking at the inspiration piece for design details, I incorporated some hand embroidery at specific points in the quilt to keep the handmade, traditional feeling.

My foot is still planted firmly in my traditional roots, but playing joyfully among its rings to make a very *me* quilt.

This quilt has been a great challenge for me. I talk often about letting go of color baggage and that I do not often use white in my quilts. Why is that? Because normally, you can add anything to white and make it look great, but I like to make my fabrics work a bit harder, so I can find the other light fabrics that will act as a white to bring the eye to the front. Playing with a color or a color combination you don't normally like is a great way to get yourself out of the creative rut. How many ways can you attack the problem until you make it work for you? This quilt took me to a whole new place of appreciation for white quilts.

But wait … is it a white quilt? I see yellow, black, cream, gold, several shades of reds and pinks—salmon, coral, tomato red, and so on. Is it really a white quilt? Or am I still just fooling myself? *Wink.*

IDEAS CARRIED OVER
from *A Summer's Day* (page 59)

▸ Being inspired not just by my grandmother's quilts but also by her other admirable crafts

▸ Crochet work and flowers

THE GOAL

▸ Make a quilt based on the lace doily made by my grandmother.

▸ Make myself use whites and light fabrics.

ADD LAYERS

▸ Add a second design element within the Double Wedding Ring—arcs, petals, dots. Find elements that can bring the quilt up a notch in design.

▸ Collect lace print fabrics.

▸ Add some vintage fabrics.

PUSH IT FURTHER

▸ Commit to the design of the lace.

▸ Design and piece the outer border of the quilt instead of just simple red solid arcs.

▸ Think about backing choices, binding, and sleeve elements from start to finish.

▸ Have fun designing your own pattern.

Remembering
CHRISTMAS PAST

There is no doubt … Minnesota winters are cold—and snowy. Did I mention cold? I remember piling into the car to drive the four hours from central Minnesota to the southeastern edge of the state to the sweet town of Wabasha to visit my grandparents. You may have seen the movie *Grumpy Old Men*, right? That movie was based on two old-timers living in Wabasha, Minnesota.

I felt I did not need to push the design much more than that. Each ring is filled with a memory.

Christmas was a fabulous time to be at my grandparents' house. Besides the house smelling of my favorite sugar cookies shaped like Santas and reindeer, they always had a real Christmas tree. (On our farm, we always had an artificial tree.) I loved lying under the tree and looking up at it to see the lights shining off the old glass ornaments.

I can remember several times going to sleep on Christmas Eve with no snow on the ground, only to wake up to three feet of snow blanketing everything in sight! I was pretty convinced that Santa had provided the gifts and the snow so we could have that white Perry-Como-cardigan-wearing Christmas. That album is still my favorite Christmas recording!

My Christmas memories are old floral drapes, glass tree ornaments, vintage cut-'n'-sew craft panels, Arthur Rankin animation like *Rudolph*

and *Frosty the Snowman*, Roy Rogers and Dale Evans horse prints that hung on the wall, feed sacks in the kitchen, the "Mary in the bathtub" covered in snow, and those giant multicolored Christmas lights that covered the pine tree in the yard. Focus fabrics were used in the centers of the rings to reflect all these memories, allowing the beauty of family Christmas traditions to stand firmly in a traditional pattern.

I felt I did not need to push the design much more than that. Each ring is filled with a memory. The scrappy-pieced, red-and-green arcs around the edge of the quilt resemble the felt garlands that hung in our house and wrap it all up in a pretty package.

Finding this vintage cowboy fabric and my grandparents' glass ornaments sent me down memory lane. What memories can you tap into, to make your own memory quilt?

Find the exact prints that fill each memory that you have, or—

▸ Make your own fabric by having it printed at Spoonflower (spoonflower.com) or on your home printer.

▸ Add photos.

▸ Add sequins and beads.

▸ Find the felt and fun fur to top off Santa's hat.

Whatever it is, find a way to add exactly what you remember and make your own family memory quilt. Each ring will hold a story for you to pass on. Be sure to label the quilt with your story, so no one will ever forget.

IDEAS CARRIED OVER
from *Lace* (page 68)

▸ Focus on the edges of a Double Wedding Ring.

THE GOAL

▸ Preserve the traditional Double Wedding Ring quilt pattern.

ADD LAYERS

▸ Make it a memory quilt.

▸ Find fabrics that represent those amazing childhood Christmases at my grandparents' house.

PUSH IT FURTHER

▸ If you can't find it, make it. Make fabrics to convey the exact feeling.

Remembering Christmas Past by Victoria Findlay Wolfe, quilted by Linda Sekerak, 2013, 78″ × 78″

FABRIC REQUIREMENTS

- **Polka dot fabric:** 1¾ yards for melons

- **Red:** 1 yard for pieced arcs and squares

- **Green:** 1 yard for pieced arcs and squares

- **Light prints:** 3¾ yards total of fat quarters and large scraps for arcs

- **Large-scale/novelty prints:** 25 squares, 13″ each for background squares

- **Red print:** 1 yard for binding

- **Backing:** 7½ yards

- **Batting:** 88″ × 88″

CUTTING

Arcs:

- Cut 92 arcs from assorted light prints, using Remembering Christmas Past solid arc pattern N (pullout page P1).

- Cut 112 red and 112 green pieces, using Remembering Christmas Past arc wedge pattern M1 (pullout page P1).

- Cut 8 red and 20 green left end wedges, using Remembering Christmas Past left-end wedge pattern M2 (pullout page P1).

- Cut 20 red and 8 green right end wedges, using Remembering Christmas Past right-end wedge pattern M3 (pullout page P1).

Squares:

- Cut 60 red and 60 green squares, using Remembering Christmas Past square pattern O (pullout page P1).

Melons:

- Cut 60 melons from polka dot fabric, using Remembering Christmas Past melon pattern P (pullout page P1).

Background squares:

- Cut 25 background squares from assorted print squares, using Remembering Christmas Past background pattern Q (pullout page P1).

Binding:

- Cut 9 strips 2½″ × width of fabric from red print fabric for binding, or make 335″ of bias binding.

Piecing

Piece the quilt according to Basic Double Wedding Ring Construction (page 102). Make a total of 60 pieced melons, referring to the quilt photo for placement of the 28 pieced arcs.

Quilt Construction

1. Construct the quilt according to Basic Double Wedding Ring Construction (page 102).

2. Quilt and bind.

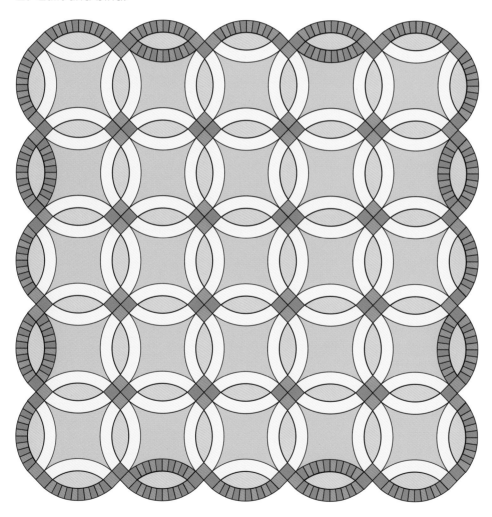

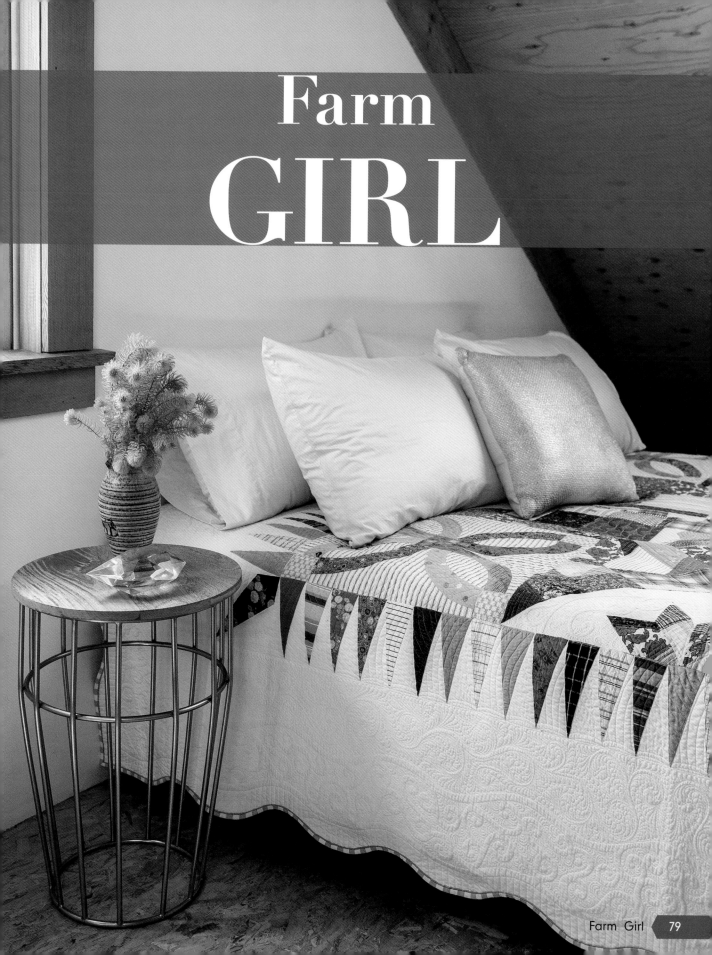

Farm
GIRL

When I left the farm, way back in the late 1980s, I didn't think anything I learned growing up there would do me any good as an artist. I practically counted the days until I could leave and head off for the big city. Even though I needed to leave to find myself, I never did stray too far from that inner farm girl—from my first vehicle, a red pickup truck, to wearing out every pair of blue jeans I ever owned. When I moved to New York City, I struggled to find my way, even though the city had a country radio station! I bought houseplants to make up for not having a garden. As soon as I got married, I started a garden and planted as many tomato plants as I could, because nothing tastes better than homegrown tomatoes.

I am still a denim girl, I ride my Harley through the streets of NYC, and I might even grow some lettuce and can 300 pounds of tomatoes every year. I am still that farm girl deep inside. It has taken quilting to get me to realize the gratitude I have for where I grew up, to look back and find my happy memories, to change my way of thinking about the things I thought I was veering away from.

Now, I hope beyond all that my New York City–raised daughter will eventually find her way to being the maker that she is. Perhaps she will build buildings, or design and engineer something new and interesting.

It has taken quilting to get me to realize the gratitude I have for where I grew up.

I know now that finding joy in quilting has brought joy to all aspects of my life. I may be living in the Big Apple, but I still put my jeans on one leg at a time and can still get the good earth under my nails… and if I am covered in threads along with it, all the better.

When I was thinking about how I could approach making the quilt that best represented me, I had to dig back to my college days, when I made my first two art quilts. They were highly criticized in the art circles as being craft, not art. But funny enough, it was in college that I had a massive seed planted about quilts.

One of my writing teachers in college was Native American, and during our semester of writing poetry and short stories, his father-in-law passed away. He invited the entire class to the wake. We all loved him as a teacher, so we all went to show our support.

I walked in, scanned the room, and saw that the plain pine box holding the body was wrapped in a beautiful Morning Star quilt. I remember sitting there, taking in the whole event, and being so struck by the quilt. The idea of being wrapped in a beautiful hand-made quilt, a last hug—I have never forgotten it. From that very moment, I thought about what the quilt I would be wrapped in would look like. I have made many star quilts over the years, each time wondering, will this be the one? None have been just right, or not quite *me*.

I started with a quilt top, or yardage of Made-Fabric, and then played out all my options before finding my direction.

I say I made this quilt from 2011 to 2014 because I made a quilt top for a completely different project, cut it apart, and never finished it. You can see here that I had many, many thoughts that never came to fruition. By playing out all the options, I was able to pull it all together into a cohesive design.

Years later, I went back and pulled out this big star quilt top again and looked at it with new eyes. I knew this quilt was going to include a Double Wedding Ring pattern in it somehow, and many other fun piecing ideas, because I am so drawn to incredibly complicated quilts. But where and how could I make it all come together?

Here the white and the quilting take the quilt to a whole new level. I do quilt some of my quilts, but I loved the idea of sharing the experience by adding quilters and their part of the story to my quilts. Karen McTavish's work on this is breathtaking.

I could have played up the piecing, or cut apart the stars even more, but I really wanted the star to dominate and the rings in the background to represent all those full-circle moments I've had in my life that got me to where I am today … keeping it real, adding blue jeans and the pink of my childhood

bedroom, using shirtings from my family's recycled clothing and even the shirt off Ricky Tims's back. I tried to incorporate all the happy moments in my life that can best tell my story. When it came time to decide whether I would quilt this myself or send it out, I asked Karen McTavish if she would do the honors. Karen is from Minnesota. She lives near where I did for a portion of my life there, and we have had many connections by way of interesting circumstances that have nothing to do with quilting, yet here we are. Life is full of full-circle moments. One must be open to having them and recognizing them, and when it happens, it is an "Aha!" moment, much like when I make creative connections when building a quilt. Maybe this will be my burial quilt. Today it seems to fit the bill.

Farm Girl by Victoria Findlay Wolfe, quilted by Karen McTavish, 2011–2014, 98″ × 98″

IDEAS CARRIED OVER

▶ More orphan play, and thoughts on who I am

THE GOAL

▶ Make a quilt that shows completely who I am—a blue-jeans-and-diamonds kind of girl. I love my country roots and adore NYC and the bling that comes with it—add a variety of fabrics beyond cotton, like denim, voile, Japanese flannel, and gold pressed linen.

ADD LAYERS

▶ Having had a lifelong goal to make the quilt I will be buried in, I think this quilt is the one.

▶ Add fabric bits that represent my life and what brings me joy.

▶ Take a traditional pattern, add some vintage and modern fabric, clothing from family and friends.

▶ Add paper piecing for the pieced border and allow it to be a white quilt, even though blue and brown are my two favorite quilt colors!

PUSH IT FURTHER

▶ Add gold piping in the binding.

▶ Keep adding new skills to your quilts!

▶ Think about how to change up the quilting. I offered it to Karen to add her story to the quilt. I can learn a lot by having someone else quilt my quilts.

▶ Add a shaped border to really make it feel classic and timeless.

▶ Have fun designing your own pattern.

Iris by
NIGHT

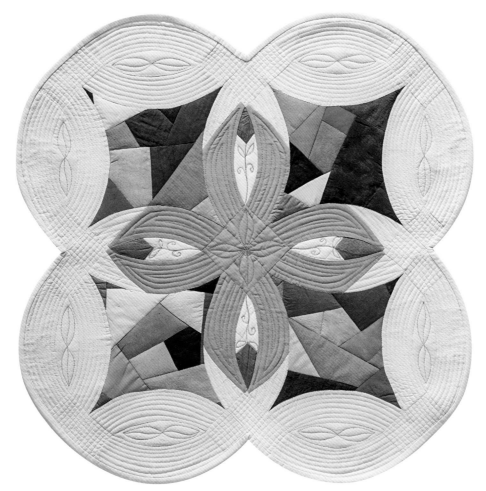

Field of Flowers, Victoria Findlay Wolfe, 2013, 28″ × 28″

When I see this photo of my grandparents, I fondly recall them standing in their garden with yellow blossoms all around them. I am lucky to have some of their original bulbs that bloom at my house every summer.

I really wanted to make a quilt based on this image of my grandparents. They were my favorite people in my life, and I miss them dearly.

For my playful sample quilt, *Field of Flowers*, I changed two things in the Double Wedding Ring pattern. I wanted to make the center concave-square shape stand out as a flower. I manipulated the small melon and the arc to represent flower buds and leaves, and just loved how the design was changed so fabulously by those two small changes.

I knew right away that the quilt needed to be made bigger! (Have you seen me? I'm tall… I need *big* quilts.)

Elda and Leo in their garden, admiring the irises

Using Cherrywood Fabrics, I played with my scraps to make a colorful batch of blooms. Looking at a pattern and asking, "What else can I do to change up the pattern?" boosts your creative process.

I love my grandparents and four-block quilts. Choosing things you love is a great place to start when deciding how to develop a new idea. What style of quilts do you love to make? Use that as a starting point and decide how you can combine the two ideas.

> *Choosing things you love is a great place to start when deciding how to develop a new idea.*

I let the old image decide the color palette for me—yellow with hints of green and gray, and even a wee dollop of pink … somewhere! I spy pink in that garden photo! I knew it had to be scrappy. I liked the idea of making the flowers float, like hand-picked bundles on a patchwork field. I made all the flowers from Made-Fabric and placed them on the background. I stood back, had a good look,

and thought, *Well, it looks good, but it needs some separation between the bundles and the background.* I sewed on some small lace trim, which is a great way to get quick finished edges! I could now tack the bundles in place and machine straight stitch them down. Easy!

IDEAS CARRIED OVER
from *Farm Girl* (page 79)

▸ Work with an older idea.

▸ Break up the basic pattern with other design elements.

THE GOAL

▸ Make a quilt that captures the feeling and memory of my grandparents, based on the photo.

ADD LAYERS

▸ Break the image apart; change the layout and style of the traditional Double Wedding Ring.

PUSH IT FURTHER

▸ I was on a mission to make more small quilts and try more and more different ways to change the pattern.

▸ Show that no matter what kind of fabrics you use, you can make Made-Fabric look interesting and fun!

▸ Add lace trim.

▸ Work with what isn't working; add elements and color.

▸ Play up the binding and backing to finish the story.

Blue Ring, Victoria Findlay Wolfe, 2013, 18½˝ × 18½˝

I changed one simple element of the fabric placement—it makes a big difference in the design!

Mary's Chicken, Victoria Findlay Wolfe, 2013, 18½˝ × 18½˝

I walked into Mary Koval's shop one day, and I saw her great display of stuffed chickens. They inspired me to play with her fabrics, and well, sometimes you just have to make a really cute chicken! Use whatever kind of fabrics you normally use. My quilts may be brighter than yours, but that is just what I have to work with. Making fabric from scraps works with whatever stash you have!

Sonnet Ring, Victoria Findlay Wolfe, 2013, 17˝ × 17˝

To use up all my tiny scraps, I decided to place Made-Fabric in the concave square and the small melons. To change things up, I pieced my arcs, and have yet another, different interpretation of the Double Wedding Ring.

Iris by Night by Victoria Findlay Wolfe, quilted by Shelly Pagliai, 2014, 75¾″ × 75¾″

Double Wedding Ring Quilts—Traditions Made Modern

FABRIC REQUIREMENTS

- **Medium to dark gray:** 3¾ yards total (each print at least ⅓ yard) for background squares

- **Light gray:** 3¾ yards total of a variety of prints for arcs, squares, small melons, leaf arc backgrounds, and bud sections

- **Lime green:** 1 yard for leaf arcs

- **Light lime green:** ⅛ yard for squares

- **Light teal:** ⅛ yard for squares

- **Dark teal:** ⅛ yard for squares

- **Light pink:** ⅛ yard for buds

- **Yellow prints:** 16 squares 10″ × 10″, plus scraps to create Made-Fabric for background squares

- **Striped fabric:** ¾ yard for binding

- **Backing:** 7¼ yards

- **Batting:** 86″ × 86″

- **Crochet lace trim:** 12 yards yellow ⅜″ wide

CUTTING

Background squares:
- Cut 33 squares 11¼″ × 11¼″ from medium to dark gray prints.

Arcs:
- Cut 64 arcs from assorted light gray prints, using the AccuQuilt arc pattern (pullout page P1).

Squares:
- Cut 80 squares from assorted light gray prints, using the AccuQuilt small square pattern (pullout page P1).

- Cut 8 light lime green, 4 light teal, and 4 dark teal squares, using the AccuQuilt small square pattern (pullout page P1).

Melons:
- Cut 32 melons from assorted light gray prints, using the AccuQuilt small melon pattern (pullout page P1).

Leaf arcs:
- Cut 32 leaf arcs from lime green, using Iris by Night leaf arc pattern R1 (pullout page P1).

- Cut 32 leaf arc backgrounds from assorted light grays, using Iris by Night leaf arc background pattern R2 (pullout page P1).

Melon buds:
- Cut 16 buds from pink, using Iris by Night bud pattern S1 (pullout page P1). Cut 16 sets of bud S2 and S3 from light gray, using Iris by Night bud patterns S2 and S3 (pullout page P1).

Background squares:
- Cut 16 background squares from yellow Made-Fabric, using the AccuQuilt background pattern (pullout page P1).

Binding:
- Cut 9 strips 2½″ × width of fabric from the striped fabric.

Piecing

The pieced iris melons must go together before you can sew anything else.

1. Piece bud S1 to bud S2; then stitch the pieced pair to bud S3 for a total of 16 buds.

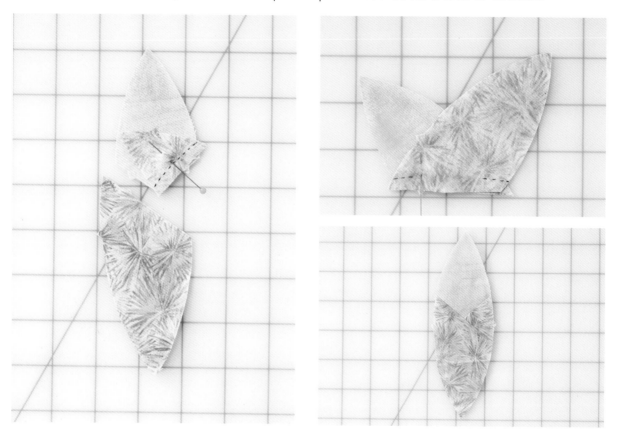

2. Piece the leaf arcs to the background leaf arcs for a total of 32 leaf sections.

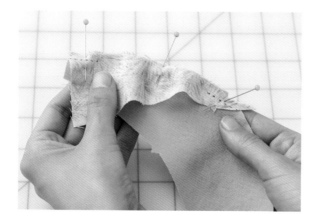
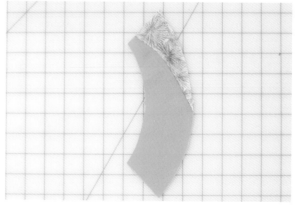

3. Piece the sections according to Basic Double Wedding Ring Construction (page 102), using the 32 leaf arcs, 16 bud melons, all the light gray arcs and melons, and all the small squares. Make a total of 16 bud/leaf melons and 32 gray pieced melons.

Quilt Construction

1. Construct the quilt according to Basic Double Wedding Ring Construction (page 102), making 4 small wedding ring units. Be sure the iris melons are in the center and facing in the right direction. Make 4 units.

2. Piece the background. The area behind the wedding ring iris sections has no squares, so the piecing will be a little tricky.

3. Sew 3 rows of 7 squares each.

4. Sew 12 squares into 6 pairs. Arrange 3 pairs between 2 rows, ladder style, with a pair at the left, middle, and right. Repeat on the other side of one of the rows with the remaining 3 pairs and the last row.

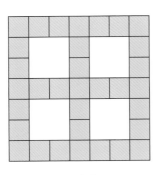

Lace

After the wedding ring sections are stitched, lace is added to the outer edges in 4 curved segments.

1. Starting at an inner corner and leaving a 1″ tail, place the lace on top of the wedding ring section, right sides together. Align the edge of the lace just over the ¼″ seamline and stitch to the next inner corner. Backstitch and cut the lace, leaving a 1″ tail. Repeat for each quadrant, overlapping the raw edges at the inner points.

2. Once it's stitched, turn the lace out so the seam allowance rolls to the wrong side of the wedding ring unit and the lace extends from the edge. Press, tucking the loose tails under to form a neat overlap.

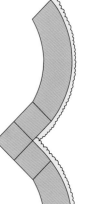

Appliqué

1. When all the lace has been applied, arrange the wedding ring units in place over the gaps in the background. Pin or appliqué glue in place and appliqué to the background.

2. Quilt and bind.

NOTE

Adding the lace makes for easy machine straight stitch appliqué. A speedy finish!

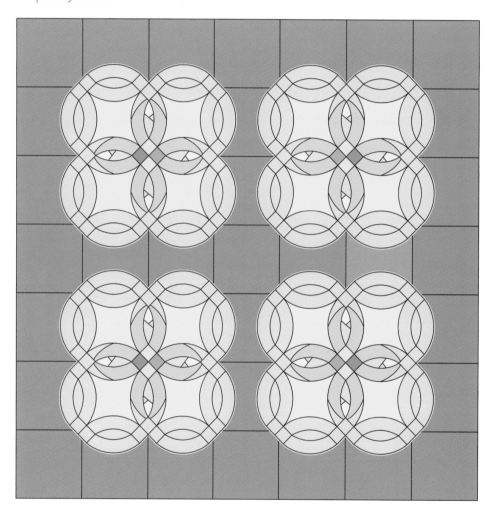

Luminous VIEWS

Luminous Views by Victoria Findlay Wolfe, quilted by Lisa Sipes, 2014, 67″ × 67″

Once I started playing with making new Double Wedding Ring patterns and incorporating more piecing, I wanted to see what would happen if I completely blew out, or fish-eyed, the whole design. I wanted to go full out, big, bold, and modern! I wanted to really play up the style in solids, to see just what I could do to make the pattern new and unique. I can tell you just from my own play in pulling apart these curves, this has given me a whole new love for exciting curved piecing!

Taking the time to learn to sew curves—pinning, pressing seams open, and watching how the fabric behaves—is key to developing your quilting skills. Take the time to try a new skill today. Each time you do, more ideas will grow!

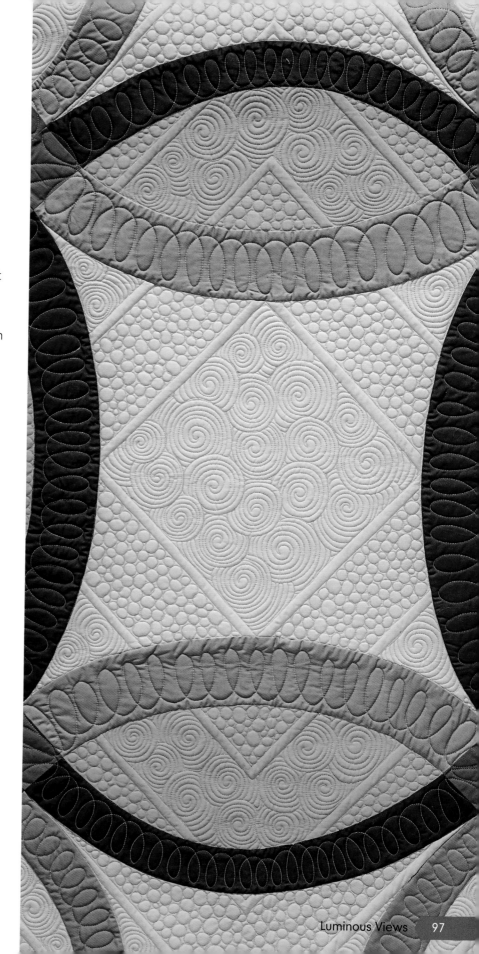

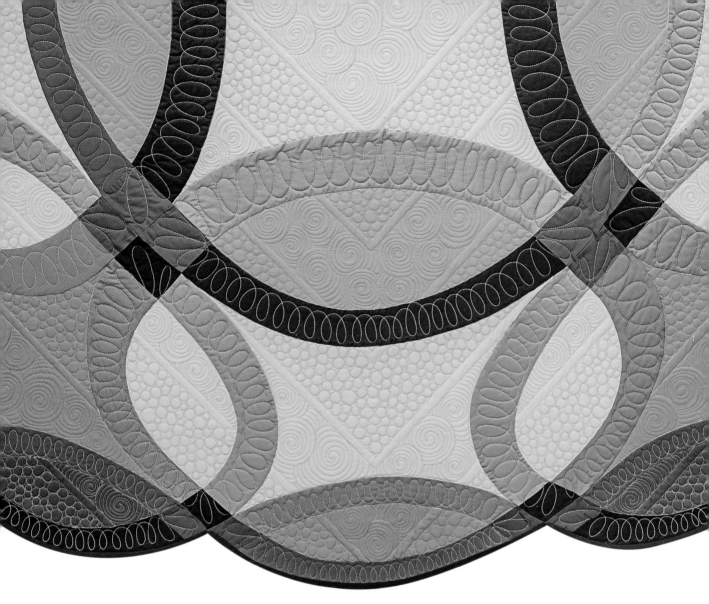

IDEAS CARRIED OVER
from *Iris by Night* (page 86)
▶ Stretch the Double Wedding Ring pattern.

THE GOAL
▶ Use only solid fabrics; explore changing the shape of the pattern.

ADD LAYERS
▶ Play with free-form curves; then draft a pattern and add seam allowances—the sky is the limit!

PUSH IT FURTHER
▶ Is anything left? Sometimes letting someone else quilt your quilts can be a great learning experience as well. Share the process, add to the story, and try something new!

▶ Have fun designing your own pattern.

WRAP UP

I hope that by now your head is swimming with ideas and your courage has been built up so that you can create your own beautiful, classic Double Wedding Ring quilt. Slow down, make your own choices, and try something new.

Dig out the old quilt tops that you lost your sewing mojo on. Take them out, shake them open, and look at the possibilities that may be there! How can you breathe new life into them? Some of my favorite quilts are ones that were made into quilt tops, cut apart, and became something completely different. *You have more fabric!* Cut them up! You can do it, and I give you permission to play!

Life is too short to worry about quilting mistakes. Embrace them. Call it a design challenge and start making quilts with soul!

Find an inspiration fabric, follow the path of information of at least three things you like, and build on it. The more you play, try, and learn, the more ideas and creative connections and "Aha!" moments you will have. Think about your story. Think about your favorite quilts. Think about how you can create something that crosses the boundaries of old and new, art, traditional and modern. The sky is the limit.

Now is the time to play!

What the Double Wedding Ring holds for me is a very personal journey that has been explored rather by accident and has now come full circle. The outcome is a truer version of myself. I love that quilts can do that! They teach us about ourselves, they bring us comfort and joy, and they have brought me together with people whom I might never have met. Does it get any better than that?

My journey to get here has been a long and winding road—not always on smooth pavement, mind you … but the bumps have made me who I really am. Now that I can see the *joy* in my life and have that respect for where I came from, I can easily say I have found my joy.

When I get to hand a quilt to someone who has nothing, I can tell you it is the best feeling in the world and when I feel I am the most "me" I will ever be.

Gratitude is habit. I am conscious of being grateful each day.

Be grateful, give back, and do not forget to play. Without joy and laughter there is no passion … be passionate!

Tell a story through fabric. Make quilts. They warm the soul.

Basic Double Wedding Ring Construction

Use a ¼″ seam allowance.

MAKING PIECED ARCS

If your project calls for pieced arcs, sew the segments together, matching the tops and bottoms of the pieces, so the resulting arc is the correct shape. Be sure to use the correct number of segments needed for each arc.

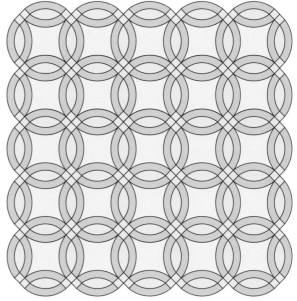

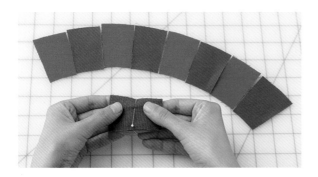

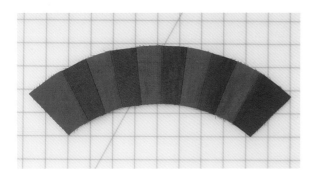

NOTE

The end pieces of the arcs will often be a slightly different pattern piece than the center segments. Refer to the specific pattern for guidance.

JOINING THE ARCS TO THE SMALL MELONS

TIP *Template plastic is great to have handy. You can see through the templates and visually get an idea of what your blocks and shapes will look like before you cut them out.*

1. Fold an arc and a small melon in half and lightly finger-press the fold to mark the center of the inner curve.

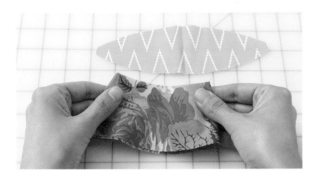

2. Place the arc and the small melon right sides together, matching the centers, and secure with a pin.

Match centers.

3. Pin the ends, easing the fabric between the pins.

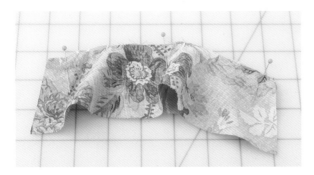

4. Sew this curved seam. This seam is easier to sew with the arc on top. For curved seam success, go slowly and lift the presser foot after every few stitches to readjust the fabric fullness.

Melon sewn to arc

TIPS FOR PIECING CURVES

- *Find the centers and pin.*

- *Pin the ends.*

- *Ease the fabric between pins.*

NOTES

- When you are working with curves, take the time to pin. It will make it easier to piece, and you will get better results. If the curves don't match properly, you will have a wavy, wiggly quilt top.

- Tight curves? Clip the seam allowances to get the fabric to relax. Press the seam allowances open or to one side, depending on the color of fabric. With the white setting fabric, press to the darker fabric.

5. Sew a square on each end of another arc.

6. Find the centers of this second arc by folding in half and finger-pressing, as in Step 1.

7. Place this arc right sides together with the first melon-arc, matching the centers, and place a pin in this spot. Pin as in Step 3, matching the ends.

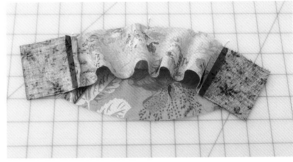

NOTE

The seams cross each other at different angles, so they will intersect only ¼″ from the edge of the fabric.

8. Sew these 2 units together to complete the pieced large melon.

9. Piece all the large melons.

CONSTRUCTING THE ROWS

1. Sew a completed melon to each side of a background square or diamond using the same pinning and stitching technique you used to make the melons.

2. Add a background piece to the bottom of this block.

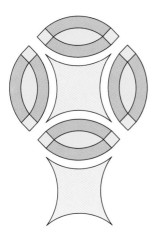

3. Continue this process to sew the units into either straight or diagonal rows, depending on the desired setting.

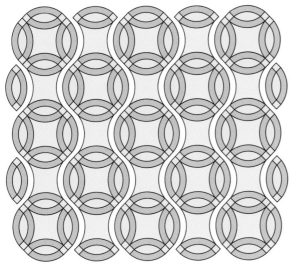

Straight set; vertical rows

On-point set; diagonal rows

SEWING THE ROWS TOGETHER

Sew the curvy rows together, matching the centers and using the same pinning and stitching technique you used previously.

TIP *Don't be afraid of these long S-shaped curved seams. As you sew, stop and lift the presser foot to adjust the fabric fullness every few stitches; then lower the presser foot and continue sewing. This will help you avoid stretching or pleating.*

Photocopy this page to design your quilt.

Photocopy this page to design your quilt.

Basic Made-Fabric and Slashing Techniques

MAKING MADE-FABRIC

1. Choose a handful of scraps. Try to refrain from cleaning up the edges, unless you just can't sew a straight seam without straightening the edges.

2. Pick up a scrap and sew a second scrap onto one of its sides.

3. Trim the seam allowance to ¼˝. Press the seam allowance to the side.

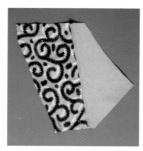

4. Keep adding bits of fabric until the piece is larger than the template pattern piece you want to use it for—on and around, here and there—pressing and trimming the seam allowance as you add each piece.

NOTE

If your piece requires only Made-Fabric, trim the Made-Fabric using the appropriate template pattern referred to in the project instructions. If it requires Made-Fabric and slashing, make and add the slashing before trimming the pieces.

SLASHING TECHNIQUES

1. Slash the fabric into 2 pieces.

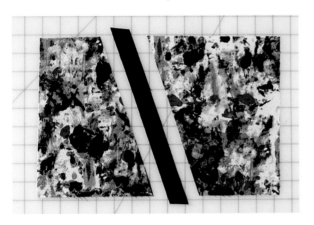

2. Sew these pieces back together with a strip of fabric between them. Press.

3. Slash the fabric into 2 pieces again.

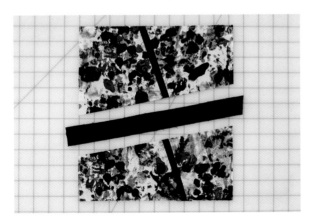

4. Sew a strip of fabric to only the top section. Press.

5. Slash the bottom section.

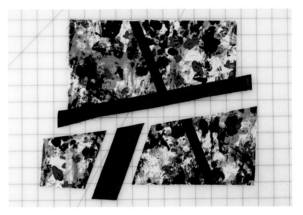

6. Sew these pieces back together with a strip of fabric between them.

7. Sew the top and bottom sections together.

8. Continue slashing and adding strips until you have a piece larger than the pattern piece you want to use it for.

9. Trim using the appropriate pattern.

Basic Paper Piecing

1. Place a background strip and a spike strip right sides together, with the background fabric on top and the long edges aligned.

2. Place the pattern, printed side up, on top of the strips, with the long edges of the strips ¼″ beyond the first diagonal line on the pattern.

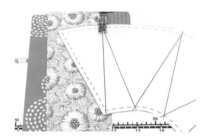

3. Stitch on the line and press to the side.

4. Fold the pattern back on the next diagonal sewing line.

5. Trim, leaving a ¼″ seam allowance beyond the folded pattern.

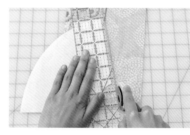

6. Align the next background strip with the previously cut edge.

7. Stitch on the line and press to the side.

8. Trim as in Step 4 and add the next spike strip.

9. Continue this process to complete the paper-pieced arc.

10. Trim around the edge of the pattern.

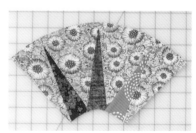

Also by Victoria Findlay Wolfe:

Victoria Findlay Wolfe is a New York City–based award-winning quilter, fabric and thread designer, teacher, and author of *15 Minutes of Play—Improvisational Quilts*. She is the founder of New York City Metro Area Modern Quilt Guild (a.k.a. NYC MOD quilters), serves as a board member of the International Quilt Association and the Quilt Alliance, and runs several community drives with Bumble Beans BASICS. She is currently the modern contributor to *The Quilt Life* magazine and has been published in many quilting industry and home magazines.

She is excited to share her series of Double Wedding Ring quilts, including the QuiltCon Best in Show, *Double-Edged Love*, as it promotes gratitude for this long-standing art form of quiltmaking.

Born and raised on a farm in Minnesota, she credits her quilting influences to her grandmother's double-knit crazy quilts that kept her warm growing up. Her biggest supporters are her husband and daughter.

Read more about Victoria at vfwquilts.com and www.15minutesplay.com.

stashBOOKS®

fabric arts for a handmade lifestyle

If you're craving beautiful authenticity in a time of mass-production...Stash Books is for you. Stash Books is a line of how-to books celebrating fabric arts for a handmade lifestyle. Backed by C&T Publishing's solid reputation for quality, Stash Books will inspire you with contemporary designs, clear and simple instructions, and engaging photography.

ctpub.com